BY DEVIL'S LUCK

To all my friends from the Polish Underground Army and in particular to those boys and girls who lost their young lives fighting, or in concentration camps and jails during the German occupation of Poland and in the Warsaw Rising of August–September 1944.

A TALE OF
RESISTANCE IN
WARTIME WARSAW

BY DEVIL'S LUCK

Stanislaw
Likiernik

MAINSTREAM
PUBLISHING

EDINBURGH AND LONDON

ACKNOWLEDGEMENTS

My thanks go to my wife, my daughter and son and to Marie
Maldague, without whose encouragement this book would never
have been written. Thanks also to Claude Roy and Witold
Zalewski, the French and Polish writers who made me understand
that my memories could be of interest to others. Special thanks to
Stefan Waydenfeld and Daunta Likiernik Waydenfeld for all the
work they have put into the translation and editing of this book.
Many thanks to Professor Norman Davies for kindly
writing the foreword to this book.

First published in Great Britain in 2001 by
MAINSTREAM PUBLISHING COMPANY (EDINBURGH) LTD
7 Albany Street
Edinburgh EH1 3UG

ISBN 1 84018 397 7

A catalogue record for this book is available
from the British Library

Typeset in Bodini Classic and Stempel Garamond
Printed and bound in Great Britain by
Butler and Tanner Ltd, Frome and London

Contents

FOREWORD 7

INTRODUCTION 9

1. HAPPY YEARS 11

2. POLAND BEFORE THE SECOND WORLD WAR AND THE JEWISH
PROBLEM 19

3. THE CLATTER OF GERMAN BOOTS 29

4. GERMAN INVASION, WAR AND ANOTHER PARTITION OF POLAND 35

5. WARSAW UNDER OCCUPATION. THE ARREST OF MY FATHER 41

6. THE DAWN OF THE UNDERGROUND. THE ONSET OF PERSECUTION 49

7. THE HARD DAYS OF OCCUPATION 57

8. MY LOVES, MY FRIENDSHIPS AND SABOTAGE 65

9. THE WARSAW GHETTO. MY WORK IN THE PFEIFFER TANNERY 75

10. THE UNDERGROUND AS A WAY OF LIFE 81

11. A GERMAN VISIT. A BOTCHED JOB 91

12. THE MOST ELEGANT OF KEDYW'S OPERATIONS 95

13. A BUSY DAY 99

14. THE ARREST OF WACEK AND HIS MOTHER.
GHETTO RISING AND ITS LIQUIDATION 105

15. JULY 1944: RED ARMY AT THE GATES OF WARSAW 111

16. THE WARSAW RISING 1 (1 AUGUST 1944) 113

17. THE WARSAW RISING 2 (11 AUGUST 1944) 121

18. THE WARSAW RISING 3 (29 AUGUST 1944) 129

19. THE WARSAW RISING 4 (CZERNIAKÓW) 139

20. THE WARSAW RISING 5: THE SURRENDER
(2 OCTOBER 1944) 147

21. THE 'LIBERATION': 17 JANUARY 1945. FAMILY REUNIONS 149

22. AFTER THE WAR. THE POLISH PEOPLE'S REPUBLIC   155
23. TO FREEDOM ACROSS EUROPE   163
24. PARIS – ANOTHER WORLD   173
25. SETTLING IN   181
26. ANNIE   189
     EPILOGUE   195
     POSTSCRIPT   199
     TRANSLATORS' NOTE   203
     INDEX OF PSEUDONYMS AND NAMES   205

Foreword

Sixty years after the Second World War, the British and American public remains poorly informed about many aspects of the conflict which moulded developments in Europe for the rest of the twentieth century. We tend to possess small, selective islands of knowledge, which serve to reinforce our own rather parochial view of the war as seen from the West. In particular, wc tend to believe that all the evil of the war emanated from our enemy, the Nazi Reich, and that all the occupied countries were, in the end, 'liberated'.

Stanisław Likiernik's memoir, whilst recounting episodes of extraordinary courage and sacrifice, will help readers to reflect on some of the realities as opposed to the myths. Born into a secure and patriotic family in pre-war Warsaw, he presents an eye-witness account of the fate of his native city, the capital of the country, for whose defence and independence the Allied cause was first formed. The narrative moves from the Blitzkrieg of 1939 to the Ghetto Rising of 1943, the main Warsaw Rising of 1944 and Hitler's chilling order to have the entire rebel city destroyed. Much of it is concerned with Likiernik's own activities in *Kedyw*, the sabotage and diversionary section of the Home Army (AK), which owed its allegiance to the exiled government in London and which was largely trained by Britain's SOE. It ends with the wounded author's successful escape to the West at a time when Poland was falling into the clutches of a Stalinist dictatorship and when other survivors of the wartime Resistance were being ruthlessly killed by the victorious Soviets. Despite unparalleled heroism, justice, democracy and freedom did not triumph.

Norman Davies
2001

Introduction

Since their early teens my son and daughter have kept asking me to record my memories. To our great regret, my father, whose life had been extremely eventful, had not done so and thus they pressed me not to repeat his mistake.

I started writing this memoir on 14 June 1978, when my son turned twenty-one, and, to my great surprise, writing about my childhood proved to be a great pleasure. Remembering that happy and carefree time in independent Poland was a joy in itself and words flew easily from my pen, almost without hesitation. And then I came to a halt – I reached the year 1939 and was not able to continue.

I thought deeply: did I have to cross that watershed? Did I really need to delve into the black years of the German occupation? How stressful would it be? At what cost to my emotional life? Or would it be wiser to let the ghosts of the past stay buried for ever?

And then, some fifteen years later, in November 1993 to be exact, when consulting a doctor made me suddenly and acutely aware of my mortality, I realised that if I meant to write about the dark time of my life it would have to be done now or never. That if, unlike my father, I was to share my experience with my children and with my grandchildren, I had to knuckle down and write not only about that difficult time in Poland during the Second World War which had made me what I am now, but also about the lesson I have learned: that a slave's life is not worth living, while freedom is worth fighting and dying for. Thus the decision was made and the book has since been published in French and also translated into Polish and published in Poland.

ONE

Happy Years

'THE EARTH IS SPHERICAL, LIKE AN ORANGE,' my father concluded his discourse. In my three-year-old mind I instantly knew what he meant: you have to dig a hole in the ground and in it you will discover an orange, and on the other side of that orange you will find Australia. I dug a hole at least twenty centimetres deep. There was no orange. I gave up. But the image remained.

This episode, the earliest memory of my childhood, comes with the scent of horses, the shaved heads of enlisted men, the shiny swords and the ringing spurs of the officers of the First Regiment of Horse Riflemen who were witness to my birth in the garrison town of Garwolin.

Yet another episode from these early years comes to my mind. We lived in the middle of a park in a house reserved for officers, near a large exercise field. Next door was a big rectangular building, the riding school. There we used to watch equestrian shows, jumping competitions, manoeuvres of mounted units, events in which our fathers often participated. One October afternoon I and my four-year-old friend played doctors in the riding school, in the space between the big gateway and the palisade fencing off the riding plot. My friend was the 'doctor', and to examine me he took off all my clothes. This was easy. The examination finished, I had to dress myself. The problem was that I couldn't do it without help. And my friend was no help at all. He took the easy way out and ran away. In his haste he shut the heavy main door. It was a cold autumn day. I was naked, freezing, and no help was coming. To my shame I started crying. Luckily, my cries were heard by Mrs Chojnacka, one of the officers' wives. Sobbing in the riding school? Nonsense. A hallucination. Wind in the trees . . . She was about to pass by on her way home, but then she stopped, turned back and found me, in my birthday suit, shivering with cold.

This was the first, but not the last, instance of outside intervention in my life. Call it the luck of the devil, or the grace of God . . . whatever. Much later Tina Strasburger, now Mother Superior of the Order of Immaculate Conception in Szymanów, had much to say to me about God's grace.

A colourful patchwork of such episodes, the sight of exercising cavalry units, the ill-understood soldiers' jokes, which unwittingly repeated to the maid earned me inexplicable smacks on the bottom, and finally that box on the windowsill – our first wireless set – telling a tale about sparrows, all form in my mind's eye a medley dancing endlessly like fragments of coloured glass in some confused kaleidoscope.

Even at that tender age, I was aware of pretty women whose scent would attract me like a bee to honey. One of these ladies – 'a really fine woman,' as my father would later say – became a great friend of mine. At the age of two I would follow her everywhere, babbling 'lovely lady, lovely lady', and, finding me irresistible, she would pick me up.

A happy, carefree, cloudless childhood. And the indelible impression of my father's glamorous uniform, his imposing moustache, his lively horse, delights me and stays with me to this day.

The officer corps of the Polish Army of the time (1925–27) consisted mainly of university or college graduates: lawyers, agronomists – like my father – civil or other engineers and many more, whose choice of a military career was largely fortuitous. They had all fought either in the First World War or in the Polish-Bolshevik war of 1920, perhaps in both, and chose to remain in the newly created army of resurrected Poland. The educational and cultural level of the corps was therefore much higher than one would expect.

Life, though on a shoe string, was full of joy. The country was free again and the army presented a handsome, almost Napoleonic sight. Splendid uniforms, well-kept horses, celebratory parades. Balls in candlelit ballrooms would end at dawn with the majestic White Mazurka. This world of my childhood belonged more to that of *War and Peace* than to the twentieth century. Moreover, my parents were people of firm, unshakeable convictions, and my universe felt secure and unassailable.

Such are the memories of my childhood and deeply rooted in them is my enduring love of horses, of the odours of the stable, and, I sheepishly admit, of a good marching song, preferably in Polish.

If any single notion dominated my upbringing at home and at school, it would best be expressed by the word 'honour'. At the age of two I learned to echo my father's dictum: 'Courage adorns both youth and virgin.' The words had become my mantra which, to the great amusement of adults, I repeated before every daring feat, taking the resultant general laughter for a sign of approval.

My father had an infinite reserve of stories. Adventures of the lovely Desdemon*ka* and her tormentor Othell*unio*, of a certain Ulyss*ek* and his horse, were a minuscule part of his rich repertoire, in which the Polish suffixes converting the names into diminutives had a surprising effect. Suitably adapted, the characters of Shakespeare's plays and Homer's heroes stayed for ever in my memory, dancing on the border of truth and fantasy, always a source of amazement, sending shivers down my back and embedding themselves in my mind.

My friendship with Roman Mularczyk, the son of one of my father's officer friends, started also about this time. Roman was two years older than I and later, especially during the Second World War, assumed an important role in my life.

Our regimental life ended in 1928 when my father was moved to the Intelligence Department of the General Staff in Warsaw and we relocated to Konstancin, a holiday resort some fifteen kilometres south of the capital. Here individual villas were scattered in pine woods, surrounded by orchards and fields of corn and potatoes. School ended in the early afternoon and the rest of the day was one long playtime. And there were plenty of safe places to play in the woods and the fields. The roads were also safe; motor cars were still a luxury even for the well-off, and in the evenings we would go riding, Father on his mare with the odd name of Gondola, and I on my filly, Baśka.

Let me now say a few words about my mother. She was a handsome woman, full of energy. She held unshakeable opinions on all aspects of life, she was invariably dogmatic, convinced of her pope-like infallibility, and she exercised an absolute authority, at least where our maid, our batman and myself were concerned. Consequently, the three of us formed a kind of united front. She also had total control over my rather henpecked father. She would thus sharply criticise his habit of drinking water with every meal: 'A glass of tea after a meal is good for you, but one must never drink while eating. Drinking water with your food is the surest road to ill-health.'

Christmas, Easter, birthdays, name-days and other anniversaries played an important role in our lives. Friendly parties, games of bridge, long walks, winter outings in sledges and later on skis, filled our leisure time. And though the modest means of a captain allowed for no extravagance, life, at least as I remember it, was happy and carefree.

The school I went to was rather unusual. It was a small private establishment run by two sisters by the name of Domański. Both were spinsters, well educated, refined, devoutly religious and dedicated to their job. They spoke perfect French. My perception of science had been conditioned very early on and almost ruined by the sight of one of these ladies trotting round the school before a storm, a little bell in her hand, ringing it to deflect thunderbolts. The bell, needless to say, came from Notre Dame de Loretto, a holy place in Italy. And the method proved to be effective: our school had never been struck by lightning.

A memorable event in my school years was the arrival of an American boy, Benjamin Hilliard, who knew no language other than his native English. His ten-year-old head was full of crazy ideas which he invariably endeavoured to put into practice. To celebrate his arrival, he climbed on to the roof of the school gazebo. In spite of the injunctions delivered in the most authoritative Polish by the two ladies, terrified by the exploits of this ape-child, he refused to come down, pretending a total inability to understand them. Naturally, inserted in this manner into our school life, the new boy enjoyed enormous popularity and his fame spread far and wide. Another source of his enduring celebrity was his possession of hundreds of glass marbles which shimmered with all the colours of the rainbow. These objects were as yet unheard of in our neck of the woods and so they were coveted by all. Games played to win even one of their finite number were a source of incomparable thrill. Our new friend learned Polish quickly, but he remained a foreigner and so he had the reputation of his country to uphold. To that end, no doubt, he was forever inventing new and increasingly frantic and daring games, impressing us all with his delightful bravado.

One of our teachers was an elderly French lady. This small in stature and hunchbacked Mademoiselle arrived in Poland as a young girl, probably engaged as a lady's companion or nanny, and had somehow stayed on in our country ever since. She dreamt of seeing *La douce France* again some day, and spoke of her *patrie* with a nostalgia which we could not begin to comprehend. She used to dine on items as strange and inedible as dandelion leaves. The French, with their taste for weeds, frogs, snails, and God only knew what else, seemed to me a very odd nation indeed. Little did I know that I would spend most of my adult life in their country.

In this context let me tell you an amusing story. I was five or six years old when my father went to Paris with an official Polish delegation. As well as a Parisian gown for my mother and some toys for me, he brought back a wealth of new stories. One was a tale of 'oysters with Chablis'. I did not quite understand it. 'What are oysters?' I asked. 'They are small sea creatures which one swallows live and whole,' Father answered and, to make the story even more fascinating, 'with Chablis, *z Chablis*,' he added. I did not need to ask what 'Chablis' meant. I knew the Polish word *szabla* (the genitive, *szabli*, being pronounced exactly in the same way as *Chablis*) meant a sword. *Z szabli* could mean only one thing: *from a sword*.

The story inevitably created in my mind's eye an image of my father swallowing oysters from a sword. This picture remained with me well into my adulthood. *Szabla*, the sword, was a very familiar object; every officer had one. But I did have a slight technical difficulty. One could easily skewer the small creatures on a sword, but given the length of the weapon, how would one eat them off it? But these were minor technicalities and without further ado I dismissed the problem.

Until one day in 1946, in Paris, in the Dupont-Latin restaurant in Boulevard Saint Michel, a friend asked me:

'Have you ever tasted oysters?'

'No, never.'

'Waiter, two dozen oysters and a bottle of Chablis, please.'

And only then the image of my father swallowing oysters *z szabli* came vividly back to my mind. To the evident amazement of my companion, I burst out laughing. But I had to agree that oysters did go down well with Chablis.

Unlike the English, most people in Poland had at least a smattering of a foreign language. My parents spoke fluent Russian and German, but when they wanted children to be excluded they would switch over to French, *pas devant les enfants* being the cue. In our milieu, familiarity with foreign languages was taken for granted and we started learning French from the age of five or six. This seemed to me natural; natural, which doesn't mean easy. Many wealthy families hired young French or German women to take care of their children. English was not widely known. Russian, the school language in my parent's time under the tsarist rule was, not surprisingly, shunned in an independent Poland and had been completely discarded by my time.

School did encroach somewhat on my daily routine, but it was not very high on the list of my priorities. My friends and I formed a secret society, mostly of boys, but we included one girl renowned for devising the craziest of schemes. We used invisible ink to communicate and we repelled our enemies with 'dust bombs' invented by Eddie Strasburger, another friend two years my senior. The bomb consisted of a paper bag filled with dust collected on sandy country tracks. Thrown at an enemy, it would burst on contact and the resulting thick cloud of dust would envelop and suffocate the adversary. However, early on in our wars it choked us as well, until Eddie invented a dust mask for our protection. The principle of the dust mask was supposed to follow that of the gas mask, though our 'filter' consisted of lumps of coal nicked in the kitchen and crushed into small fragments; this was the only kind of coal we had ever heard of.

Unfortunately, our dust mask proved to be somewhat imperfect. A boy from Warsaw joined us once in our war game. He was very keen in the beginning. He took part in our manoeuvres, threw bombs and generally exhibited the required courage, but suddenly his enthusiasm ebbed. It was only when we put our enemies to flight that we discovered the reason for his waning ardour: he had almost suffocated having actually vomited inside the mask. However, he fought heroically at our side to the bitter end.

These anecdotes appear trivial no doubt, but later, in very different circumstances, our make-believe wars, 'the heroic resistance in the face of our historic enemies', proved to have been a finely tuned preparation for our adult life.

Our rules of behaviour were unequivocal and they became our Code of Honour:

* If someone insults your country, your parents, or yourself – hit him hard!
* Never hit one weaker than yourself.
* Never hit a woman, not even with a flower.
* To betray a comrade is a crime; accept the punishment yourself instead.

We internalised these sentiments from our earliest childhood. They had been transmitted to us by our parents and teachers. From the present point of view our upbringing, steeped in the traditions of unalloyed patriotism and the heroic stories of our idealised past, seems excessively flamboyant. An explanation may be found, perhaps, in our only recently recovered independence and in the romantic poetry which inspired the nation during the 123 years of partition.

I was eight years old when on Independence Day I recited in public a poem on the glory of the young defenders of Lwów:

O, *mamo otrzyj oczy*	Oh, mother dry your eyes
Z uśmiechem do mnie mów	Speak to me with a smile
Ta krew co z piersi broczy	The blood which seeps from my breast is
To za nasz Lwów . . .	For our city of Lwów . . .

My performance was received with thunderous applause, mothers' handkerchiefs were out, even the men were close to tears.

The officer brotherhood, the world of my parents, did not seriously seek answers to such problems as the low living standard of the overpopulated countryside, the weakness of our industrial base and the low pay of the workers. These were the legacy of the partitions. All our resurrected country needed was time. The world wide economic depression made the task of recovery difficult, but our idolised Marshal Piłsudski would find a way. Perhaps the ideas of our elders were not quite as simplistic as that, but their doubts, if any, did not percolate through to my level.

❧

In 1935 I progressed from the primary to the secondary school. I sat an examination and entered the first grade of the *Tadeusz Czacki Gimnazjum* in Warsaw. This was situated near the Old City and, like my father, I spent an hour each way commuting daily to the capital. Consequently, before the New Year my parents decided to move to Warsaw.

My last memory of Konstancin is that of Władek Gordyjczuk. This twenty-one-year-old soldier doing his national service was my father's batman. He came from far away Polesie, a province of Poland bordering on the Soviet Ukraine. Polesie was known for its bogs and swampy forests, and its inhabitants, mainly Belorussian peasants, were more used to boats then to carts.

Władek was married, he had a child and became very fond of me. I remember him as a very good-natured, cheerful and rather naive young man. I vividly remember his boundless enthusiasm on first seeing the Bengal lights burning on our Christmas tree. He used to receive an occasional letter from his grandfather, the only literate member of his family. Władek himself had never learned the art of reading or writing, and could see no reason for doing so. His grandfather was literate and that was enough. I was of the opposite opinion and vowed to teach him myself. My success was only partial: he learned to sign his name. The next morning the walls of the kitchen were covered with his signature: W. Gordyjczuk. My mother did not share my delight in his achievement. Luckily, Władek had used a pencil. The next few hours he had to spend erasing his handiwork. He reached a much greater triumph in his regiment when, on some official paper and to the amazement of his sergeant, in place of the cross, customary for the illiterate, he placed his full signature. 'Jawor taught me,' he explained. *Jawor*, which is Polish for sycamore, was his affectionate nickname for me. How he came by it remains a mystery.

In those years we never went on holiday. There was no need. Father had his mare, Gondola, I had Baśka, there was a forest close by for walking and we could bathe in the nearby river, the Jeziorka. Władek was an excellent swimmer. Under his eye I learned to swim in the three square metre segment of the river sufficiently deep for the purpose.

Though an only child, I had never been lonely. For two years my mother looked after a ten-year-old girl whose parents had separated, and later after a boy of my own age, Janek Srebrny, whose mother was dead and who lived with us for over a year. While I strongly objected to the female of the species – at the age of ten I was not at all interested in the opposite sex – Janek won me over in no time and very quickly became my playmate. As well as all kinds of make-believe fights and games, we delighted in practical jokes, not always sophisticated or refined. One day, for instance, I lay motionless on the bathroom's tiled floor while Janek in a fake panic called my mother, 'Come, come quickly, Stan has slipped and is lying still on the floor! Is he dead?' Mother rushed upstairs. The surprise having been achieved, I got up and as we were preparing to laugh, to our utter astonishment, my mother, obviously devoid of any sense of humour, gave us both a good hiding.

TWO

Poland Before the Second World War and the Jewish Problem

TO LEAVE KONSTANCIN WAS PAINFUL, but its pleasant memories remained with me for a long time. Some, like the dancing lessons run in the drawing rooms of wealthy Konstancinians by Mr Sobiszewski, our maestro, who would come regularly for this purpose from Warsaw, were easy to forget. But to forget my friends, the woods and the stables was a different proposition.

The first few months in Warsaw were wretched. We moved into a three-storey block in Żolibórz, a north Warsaw suburb. Our flat, three rooms and a bathroom, cramped by present standards, was comfortable. I had my own room with a balcony. I liked the city, but as yet I had no chums in Żolibórz. The public park across the street held no attractions for me. Neither did the ice-skating rink in the winter. But the feeling of bereavement didn't last long.

Soon my school, near the Old City, became the centre of my life. Now that my own children are grown up, I can admit that my teachers classed me as a restless boy who talked too much. I had apparently some ability, but boisterousness took the upper hand and the consensus of opinion presented to my parents was of the 'could do better' variety. In spite of having to suffer their rebukes and punishments, I got on well with the teaching staff, with the exception of 'The Pyramid'. This was our nickname, justified by her shape, for our French teacher, Mme Klimaszewska. She spoke French very well, but with a strong Polish accent. I had no quarrel with that. But we did have our differences of opinion on the subject of French spelling. Now, having spent nearly fifty years in France, I must admit that hers had been faultless while mine was rather extravagant. In later life, my French wife took on the task of improving my French; it did not prove an easy undertaking, but now at least my spoken French is better then Mme Klimaszewska's ever was.

⁂

Poland in the '20s and '30s was a 'strong man democracy'. The milieu in which we lived fostered the strong man, Marshal Piłsudski and later his successors, collectively known as 'the colonels'. My father, though often critical of the government, envisaged no possibility of change to a better system. Even though the situation of the industrial worker was far less favourable than ours, it was the overpopulated countryside, home to over two-thirds of the nation, that was in the grip of extreme poverty due to the depression. Many peasants either had no land to call their own or worked a miserable, grossly inadequate plot. The system inherited from the occupying powers, Russia, Prussia and Austro-Hungary, was quasi-feudal and thousands of hectares were in the hands of large landowners; attempts at agrarian reform invariably failed. As in Spain, the church and the clergy, both extraordinarily backward, played a prominent role in the life of the country.

However, at the time I was not really cognisant of the situation. It was my country, right or wrong, now independent and free. After 123 years of foreign domination our parents had laid the foundations of the independent Poland they had fought so hard for. Ours was the first generation with a real chance to make it work.

To our east was the Soviet Union, the loathsome enemy, who had tried to strangle the resurrected country at birth and to re-impose by war the hateful Russian rule; that it was now called 'Bolshevik' did not change anything. On 15 August 1920, the newly recreated Polish army had repelled the enemy at the gates of Warsaw and pursued him far to the east. The battle came to be known as 'The Miracle on the Vistula'. Though the strategy of Marshal Piłsudski was given its due, it was overshadowed by the belief in the intervention of the Virgin Mary who was thought, for some reason, to care particularly deeply about the fate of the Polish Army.

Our idyllic image of Poland was, however, not without its shadows. My father was often critical of the strikes, the economic stagnation, the unemployment. Yet on the other hand there were Gdynia, our newly built port on the Baltic sea, and our powerful army with its magnificent cavalry and airforce.

In this atmosphere, the views of a young Jewish worker whom I engaged in conversation one day, were a considerable shock to me.

He had come to repair a piece of furniture. To my great amazement he disdained the Polish regime and admired that of the Soviet Union. I tried to argue, but his convictions were firm and while he seemed to know what he was talking about, I did not. I was certainly not converted by him, but he did sow some doubts in my mind. Perhaps not everything was quite so rosy in our garden? Perhaps not everybody was as happy and had the same beliefs as we did?

To my best recollection, the newspapers and magazines I used to browse through at home were generally supportive of our rulers, and so were we and our friends. There was an opposition of a sort in the form of the National Democratic Party, but it was even more conservative than the Piłsudski group which was actually in power. The Polish Socialist Party was legal, but had a minimal influence on the running of the country.

I do not intend to discuss in depth the socio-political background of pre-war Poland, nor am I now able to look at the past with the eyes of a thirteen-year-old boy. My opinions were inevitably remoulded, first by my experience of the Second World War and then by my years of study and life in France, the country which has become my home. And as I write these words now, at the end of the twentieth century, I cannot possibly touch dispassionately upon the Jewish problem, important as it was before the war, pretending ignorance of the momentous happenings during and after it.

In pre-war Poland the close to 3.5 million Jews accounted for about ten per cent of the country's population. They lived mostly in small or large towns and cities, and were engaged in all kinds of occupations. In commerce, in crafts and skilled trades and in the learned professions, the proportion of Jews was often much higher than ten per cent. On the other hand, in agriculture, which employed seventy per cent of the country's population, Jews were few and far between.

Jews tended to live apart, not so much because of the attitude of Poles but mainly because of their own wish not to mix with gentiles, to be among their own kind. A great majority of Polish Jews spoke Yiddish, a dialect derived from German. Their Polish was heavily accented and was often full of errors of grammar and syntax. At the same time, a part of the Jewish population, small but important because of their high intellectual achievements, had been seduced by the Polish culture and lifestyle, by the Polish language and literature. Great poets and writers, such as Julian Tuwim and Antoni Słonimski, were masters of the Polish language and were in the forefront of the literary establishment. Those intellectuals of Jewish origin who adopted Polish culture enriched it with their Jewish traditions. One of my father's French friends averred that these Judo-Slavs, as he called them, were a very successful hybrid.

In the Polish Army a few officers of Jewish origin managed to climb quite high up the service's ladder, even though their advancement was at times hindered by the prevailing anti-Semitic attitudes. My own contact with Jews had been limited to an occasional visit to the shops, the tailors or the shoemakers in the nearby village of Jeziorna.

Mr Dębski, a bespoke tailor, had a Polish name but was a typical Jewish master craftsman, serious and traditional. He made my first secondary school uniform: navy blue with silver buttons. He and his two or three apprentices, who included his own son, all worked in one room. Mrs Dębski, who would make her appearance from time to time, wore a wig covering her shaved head, a religious custom of which I was unaware at the time. Mr Dębski must have been about seventy. The silver beard which grew down to his chest gave him the solemnity of a biblical patriarch. As a child he had helped his father, also a tailor, to make uniforms for the Polish insurgents of 1863. He was a man of dignity who inspired respect.

I also used to visit the villa of Mr Morgenstern, a wealthy Jewish banker. It was one of the nicest villas in Konstancin. His son, Ryszard, had a French governess and had even once gone on holiday to the French Riviera, which impressed us, his schoolmates, immensely. It was in Ryszard's home that I learned a new expression, passed on no doubt by the said governess and totally incomprehensible either to him or to me, namely: *foumoilecamp*, as a single word. Its meaning – get lost – became clear to me only many years later.

The entire family – Mr Morgenstern, his very attractive wife, Ryszard and his little sister – were all murdered by the Nazis.

I have dwelt on the Jewish problem at some length, because just before leaving Konstancin or perhaps when I was already in Warsaw I had a shock which, I believe, coloured the rest of my life and is particularly relevant to the rest of my story.

I must have been about eleven at the time. My father was a professional soldier, an officer of the General Staff, a patriot, serving the Republic of Poland, at last independent.

In Konstancin I had many friends. Some were Catholics, others were Lutherans, still others Jewish (or of the 'Mosaic persuasion', as it was officially called). But we were all Poles, steeped in Polish culture and tradition. The father of one was a doctor, another a banker, still another a teacher. Edward's mother, a widow and a fervent Catholic, had a stable of riding horses for hire. Religion was not a problem for any of us. We were all Poles. Besides, at the time, just after my first communion, I was an ardent believer.

Jeziorna, a small village three kilometres from Konstancin, was a different world; ninety-five per cent of the population were Jewish. Bearded men, some with corkscrew curls, in long, black coats, wore round caps with small peaks. Whether skilled craftsmen, tradesmen, or shopkeepers, they formed a close religious community. On occasions I would go to Jeziorna, to the shop of Mr Lewek to buy sweets or, more often, poppy-heads. The latter had tasty contents, but their fascination lay more in the rattling noise which they made when shaken. The shop had a characteristic smell, a mixture of kerosene, food, and native and exotic fruit. A strong smell of fried onion pervaded the shop from the Lewek family kitchen behind it.

I don't know when or how, but about that time I learned that my family had Jewish roots. I believe that the sudden discovery that I might have something in common with these people, so strange and foreign, must have been a great and indelible shock for me.

In spite of the fact that my great-grandfather (1817–86) took part in the tragically crushed Polish rising against the Russians in 1863 and that my grandfather and father were great Polish patriots, suddenly, I may not have been quite the same as the others, the true Poles. And, at the age of eleven, one desperately wants to be normal, to fit in without reservations.

In time I came to terms with the problem and it had no bearing on my life before the war. But in the years 1939–45, under the German occupation, this hiccup in my curriculum vitae assumed dramatic importance. But that was still to come.

❧

Now let me tell you in some detail about my family. Of the generation preceding my father's I only knew my grandfather's brother, Artur Likiernik, Doctor of Chemistry at the University of Zürich and a Very Important Person in Silesia: director of a big factory, president of the Chamber of Commerce and personal friend of Professor Mościcki, a fellow chemist and the President of the Polish Republic. My father showed his uncle great respect and I, naturally, stood in awe of him.

My great-grandfather, Adolf, born in 1817, who took part in the

1863 rising against the Russians and whose last will and testament, dated 1882, is in my possession, had three sons. Apart from Artur they were Maurycy, a well-known ophthalmologist, and my grandfather, Stanisław, an industrialist. I still have one of his visiting cards. The pedigree of our Polishness has thus been proved by at least three generations preceding mine.

My father's brother, Kazimierz Szczerba-Likiernik, ten years his junior, joined the Polish Legion of Marshal Piłsudski at its formation in 1914. After the Second World War he headed the Department of Social Sciences of UNESCO in Paris. He died in 1969. My father's sister, Alina Wojecka, was a snobbish grande dame, who travelled abroad and was in the habit of buying clothes for her children in Paris; in time they would often be passed down to me, but I refused to wear such effeminate apparel *à la mode de Paris*. Alina was charming but self-centred, and her relations with us were rather distant.

Similarly, we had little contact with my mother's family: three sisters, of whom two were dentists in Warsaw. The third one, an Esperanto enthusiast, lived in Czechoslovakia, and there was a brother whom I had met only once. Our calls on my Warsaw aunts had a twofold purpose, social and professional, and as the latter meant dental fillings I did not enjoy them.

My maternal grandfather was never mentioned by my parents.

I was named Stanisław after my paternal grandfather. In his photograph he sports a handsome silver-grey moustache and a prominent belly. Apparently he was wealthy, had a carriage with a good team of horses and travelled a lot in France and Italy, often accompanied by either his daughter or his son, my father. I understand that when he died at the age of fifty-three, in 1911, he left his considerable fortune to my father. My grandmother died at the age of forty-six, while travelling in Berlin in 1914, just before the start of the First World War. Their marital life had not been happy.

In his younger days my father, Tadeusz, had not been a model son. At some stage he was expelled from his Russian secondary school for his part in patriotic demonstrations. He had also been punished for less honourable exploits. He was rather small for his age but exceptionally strong and absurdly brave, indeed foolhardy. Once, for a wager, he lay on the railway line until the train passed over him. He got up intact, except for holes in his trousers and his buttocks, which had been burned by hot coals dropping from the locomotive. The end result was a good hiding when the reason for the burns and the holes was discovered.

He fought his first duel over a girl in 1898. The antagonists, both about thirteen or fourteen years old, fought with fencing foils 'to the first blood'. Due to the protective buttons on the tips of the weapons, blood refused to flow. The seconds would not interrupt the duel. But as it had been taking place in the drying room of the tannery belonging to Mr Pfeiffer, an acquaintance of my grandfather, the increasing heat of the boiler switched on by the owner put an end to the fight.

Over the years, my own children have heard directly from their grandfather about his many later exploits, including the more serious duels he fought as a student of the agricultural college in Breslau (now Wrocław). His reminiscences covered the early part of the century, before 1914: the first motorcar in Warsaw, the first aeroplane, then the war and the revolution in Russia. I can still visualise my father, by then nearly eighty, in Marly-le-Roi, our home at the time, surrounded by my children, about a dozen of their playmates and their mothers, particularly the more attractive ones with whom my father still flirted, all engrossed in listening to his tales of yore.

My father was an excellent horseman, and in 1906–14 he took part in many equestrian trials. He underwent a three-month traineeship in the Viennese *Spanische Reitschule*, the admission to which was an almost impossible achievement for a foreigner. My father, having attended one of the Emperor of Austria, Franz Joseph's, weekly audiences, had managed to get from him a letter of recommendation to the *Reitschule*.

Mobilised into the Russian army in 1915, he entered the Officer School in St Petersburg and on its completion was commissioned into the Imperial Horse Guard. His unit was sent first to the Caucasus and then to Harbin in Manchuria in quest of more horses. This little excursion on horseback took him almost to the Chinese border. It was some seven or eight thousand kilometres there and back. The high point of the journey was the crossing of Mongolia in the winter at temperatures of minus forty degrees centigrade. In the open country, the almost constant snowfalls made the visibility so bad that they felt as if they were trapped in a bottle of milk. Their local guide, however, always miraculously managed to find his way to a village before nightfall.

Tales from later times included one about his escape on horseback from a pack of wolves. This happened in the Ukraine one night in 1917, during the Bolshevik revolution. At the start of the revolution the Poles conscripted into the Russian army organised themselves into the Polish Corps commanded by General Dowbór-Muśnicki. It was with this army that my father returned to Poland. The way back was barred at Krechowce by the Germans and Father's unit, the First Regiment of Uhlans, participated in the cavalry charge in which the colonel commanding the regiment was killed. The regiment added to its official designation the adjective *Krechowiecki*, while the charge became one of my father's cherished memories.

In the 1920 Polish-Bolshevik war, my father served as adjutant to General Orlicz-Dreszer. It was another cavalry war. He sustained a chest wound but the bullet, deflected by the Dowbór Corps badge, just missed his heart. I well remember the badge, a small metal cross bent by the impact of the bullet; it was lost during the Second World War.

Taken as a whole, the history of my family is rich in events, with heroic, Napoleonic overtones, full of horses, cavalry charges and duels. In fact, my father was a great admirer of Napoleon and, aided by his phenomenal memory, was an expert on the history of the Emperor's campaigns. Tales of the Napoleonic era and of the adventures of the participating Polish units remained very much alive in our family.

To return to my own story: as mentioned before, the discovery of my family's Jewish origins made a deep and lasting impression on me. I had been baptised in infancy and brought up in a Christian household. Like most children in Konstancin, I received my first Holy Communion at the age of ten and I went to church every Sunday, though more from custom than from piety and without much enthusiasm. My parents were Catholic and their wedding in 1921 had been a proper church ceremony. Their church attendance was restricted, however, to special occasions, such as Easter, Christmas and First Communion.

Suddenly, this finely balanced system of mine collapsed. The latent anti-Semitism which I had completely ignored in the past became dramatically relevant. At the time nationalistic student groups became increasingly active, abetted and apparently occasionally financed by German Nazis. Several students of my secondary school belonged to those organisations and one of them actually subscribed to *Stürmer*, the anti-Semitic Nazi journal; later he was executed as a collaborator. While I did not accept my altered situation and desperately wanted to be the same as the others, for those people my origin was far from irrelevant. My father's attitude being what it has always been and his entire *Weltanschauung* being centred on the unquestionable Polishness of our family, my belonging to a social entity other than Polish was unthinkable for me. I believe now that it was the fact of our questionable origin that made our patriotism as intense as it was and inspired my father's and his brother's exceptional bravery in both world wars. In those years, before the creation of Israel shattered this opinion, at least in Poland the words 'Jew' and 'coward' were synonymous; the brothers had therefore to prove that they had left their Jewishness behind.

Even though I found myself in an awkward situation, the attitude of my friends, for whom my origin was irrelevant, took my mind off the problem. Eventually I accepted the fact that I was 'different' and ceased to be bothered by it. Later, however, under the German occupation when the 'difference' acquired its life-threatening meaning, I had to deal with the reality, but this neither changed my views nor brought me any closer to the Jewish community, of which at no time had I ever felt a member.

One day my father and I went to visit Aunt Zosia. Our arrival happened to coincide with that of a very agitated Jewish student. He had been attacked by the nationalists who beat him up and tore up his university identity card. He was naturally furious, but after he left I tried to defend the narrow nationalistic point of view: that the number of Jews at the university was out of all proportion to the size of the Jewish minority. My aunt called me a hooligan. Father supported me and we left Aunt Zosia's flat in a huff. I did not speak to or visit her for several months. I must admit now that it was she who was in the right.

Another time, during the Spanish Civil War, influenced by nationalistic propaganda I ventured to declare in the presence of one of my father's friends that 'fortunately the fortress of Toledo is still resisting'. The abuse which this gentleman, who had just returned from Spain, heaped on my head rearranged the ideas inside it; I understood then who Franco was – an ally of Hitler. But while Spain was far away and perhaps I was not as well informed about it as I should have been, the events taking place next door, in Germany, were well known to us. Father's work in the General Staff's Department of Intelligence, German desk, gave him excellent insight into the problem and I was well placed to pick up scraps of information from his talks with my mother and his friends. I understood that father had presented a number of detailed and – as he asserted – alarming reports regarding the German army, reports which the Chief of General Staff failed to pass further up the hierarchy. I knew about the existence of the Dachau concentration camp as early as 1937. I remember the visit to our house of a man who had been arrested in Germany as a Polish agent, sent to a concentration camp and exchanged for a German spy. I vividly remember watching with fascination his mouth as he spoke; his gums were bare, all his teeth having been knocked out. Another visitor was a German officer of Jewish origin who had to flee his own country. Father helped him to settle in Poland.

THREE

The Clatter of German Boots

WAR WAS COMING. With Nazis marching through the streets of Berlin, through the towns and cities of East Prussia, and now also Vienna and Prague, we listened with foreboding to the echoes of jackboots reaching us from the west, the north and the south. In the meantime, amazingly, life continued as normal. A Boy Scout for some years, in 1938 I was made leader of a troop of seven- to eight-year-old Cubs. I would rather have led a group of older boys, say of ten or eleven years, and so was somewhat disappointed. But I soon got into the stride and became involved in organising games and trips for my charges, gaining my first experience of leadership.

I had never been abroad until the summer holidays of 1936 which I spent with my parents in Carmen Silva, Romania. We visited Bucharest and Constanza, which left me with long-lasting memories. We made an interesting four-day excursion to Istanbul. Meeting young Romanians, including a pretty girl of my age, greatly helped my French; most educated Romanians fluently spoke the language so very similar to their own.

The following year, however, I chose to go to a Scouts' camp in the south of Poland. With my parents again going to Bucharest, and this time by air – a costly and daring enterprise in those days – it was not an easy choice.

Since we had left Konstancin, our summer holidays were spent away from home, mostly in Poland and usually as paying guests in country houses, which gave me an insight into rural life and the lifestyle of the landed gentry. These people often owned sizeable properties, 400 to 500 hectares or more, but because of the prevailing low prices of agricultural produce, they rarely had two coins to rub together and were often deeply in debt, in spite of the superabundance of cheap labour.

My favoured sport, second only to riding, was skiing. At the time we used to spend our Christmas holidays in Wisła, a small town near the source of the river Vistula, or Wisła in Polish. We usually stayed in a large villa converted into a *pension*, eight kilometres from the town. I would spend whole days outdoors in the company of a local skiing champion. Endless cross-country ski runs on feathery virgin snow through fir forests silver with hoarfrost, hours-long climbs (there were no ski lifts as yet) are forever imprinted on my memory. Often, about the time of our return at nightfall, my father and his friends would be preparing to leave in a sledge for a café in the centre of the town. As there was no room for me in the sledge, I would do another sixteen kilometres skijoring on the snow-covered road.

Towards the end of our last stay in Wisła in 1938–39 I could hardly walk. My knees were aching, though miraculously the pain would disappear while skiing. On my return to school I was found to have effusion in both knees, which was attributed to the strain of excessive skiing. To the fury of my gym teacher, I had to be excused from PE. But who cared? I had enjoyed every minute of my holiday.

In the meantime, world events were spinning out of control at an accelerating rate. Starting in 1936, the occupation of Rhineland, the Austrian *Anschluss*, the occupation of the Sudetenland and, finally, the shameful treaty of Munich, gained so much notoriety that even young people like us could not fail to be affected. My father's anxiety regarding the country's lack of preparedness for the coming war was almost palpable in his conversation and, though conscious of the problem, I did not let it disturb me unduly. Wasn't our army, after all, the pride of the nation, and didn't we have a most powerful ally in France? A French propaganda film convinced me of the strength of her land forces, the impenetrability of the Maginot line and the invincibility of her fleet.

General Ironside, the British Chief of Staff who during his visit to Poland dared to express doubts as to the efficacy of our cavalry in modern warfare, was widely criticised. The popularity of Great Britain, a country about which, compared with France, we knew very little, became tarnished.

In 1938, at the time of the Sudetenland crisis, the Polish army recovered Zaolzie, a province inhabited by Poles and seized by Czechoslovakia in 1920 when our army was fighting the Bolsheviks. But the moment was ill chosen: the entire Czech airforce of over 1,000 planes, instead of finding refuge in Poland, fell straight into German hands. Our 'success' was widely celebrated. But as my father strongly disapproved of the 'adventure', I did not participate in the jubilation. Many, however, did. General Rydz-Śmigły, the Marshal of Poland, successor of Marshal Piłsudski, was a popular though inept leader and the population thoughtlessly followed.

🕭

Such then was the climate in the country in the summer of 1939 when my parents and I were leaving for holidays by Lake Dryświaty in the extreme north-eastern corner of the country, close to the Latvian border. The long train journey was followed by about twenty-five kilometres in a *britska*, a small horse-drawn carriage. The village called Bobrusz was situated in a fir forest and the *pension*, housing some twenty persons, was sited on the shore of a large lake. We had evening meals together at a refectory table, the dining room illuminated with gas lamps; other rooms had kerosene lamps. An old radio ran on batteries. Days were filled with swimming, canoeing, sailing, long horse rides and volleyball matches against Tumulin, another *pension* further up the lake. I was not a great swimmer; 200 metres was my limit and even that seemed a great exploit. There, in Bobrusz, I discovered that one could swim non-stop for an hour or more. On the evening of our arrival, the owner of the *pension*, a man who had lost an arm in the Polish-Bolshevik war, dared us to accompany him in a swim to some shallows far into the lake. We took up the challenge, fortunately attended by a rowing boat. After half an hour we reached our destination and returned, this time with me rowing.

So far I have never mentioned my relations with the other sex. At sixteen I had done some flirting, but in my fantasies girls were still more angels than humans and thus untouched by desire. It had not even occurred to me that they might like being kissed by boys. My flirting activity during bicycle rides was purely verbal, and the required kissing of ladies' hands was not exactly an erotic experience. My reticence was enhanced when a girl I had an eye on assured me that 'a kiss is a virgin's wedding'. The prospect of a wedding cooled my ardour considerably.

The discovery that our waitresses, young peasant girls, slept in a nearby barn gave us food for thought, and, naive as we were, plans were hatched. We suspected that fear of pregnancy might make the girls less approachable. It was therefore essential to get condoms. But how and where? Simply asking for them at the village chemists would have been too embarrassing. After all, the year was 1939 and things were very different then! The approach would have to be indirect. We composed a letter to the chemist which one of us wrote in an 'adult' hand: 'Dear Sir, kindly give the bearer a packet of ten condoms. Please make sure that he is unaware of the contents. With thanks, etc.' As it happened, I was the messenger. Everything went as planned. The chemist gave me the packet of 'medicine' and we were armed for action. The sequel, however, was far less successful. In the dark of night we climbed to the top of the barn and were about to approach the intended victims of our youthful ardour when, suddenly, the *pension*'s owner materialised at the top of the ladder. He must have been after his son who, naturally, was with us. Actually, I doubt that the girls would have been willing, but they never uttered a word. Anyway, we had to give up. Such was the end of our adventure.

And so, in spite of the rumblings of war, August 1939 in Bobrusz was extremely enjoyable, with all the swimming, sailing and volleyballing I was doing. Before leaving, I wrote to father, who had returned home earlier, and asked him to help me join the First Regiment of Horse Artillery. Horses, cannons, neck-breaking gallops, battery taking positions – it was to be my own Austerlitz!

Still in Bobrusz, I met a young woman, another holiday maker, a typical Polish girl as depicted in the romantic art of the nineteenth century: blonde, blue-eyed and very attractive indeed. Trying to win her over, I would go canoeing with her on the lake. She was the daughter of Professor Dziewulski, an astronomer at the University of Wilno; a year later her father, deported by the Russians, would disappear into the Soviet Gulag.

In the meantime, my father's letters from Warsaw became increasingly disquieting. He insisted that mother and I defer our return to Warsaw pending his approval. The start of the school term, due on 4 September, had been postponed until 15 September. This was a bad omen, but not something I personally objected to. Our main source of news, the radio, was packing up, the batteries were going flat. The wheezy whispers coming from the big box were often difficult to interpret. But on 23 August we just managed to understand that Germany concluded a non-aggression pact with USSR. This was astonishing. I remember actually saying that 'should the Russians remain neutral, we'll be finished'. All talk was about the coming war. Our elders, who remembered the last one, tried to make us see that war was a calamity, but for us, the young ones, the word meant a chance to demonstrate 'our heroic qualities, in keeping with our fathers' soldierly virtues . . . riding to the gates of Berlin, no less!'

In spite of Father's 'orders', Mother decided that we would after all return to Warsaw. But before that Wanda Dziewulska had invited me to come to Wilno, to stay in her parents' home. 'The town is well worth visiting,' she added. I remember saying to my mother: 'If the Russians are allied to Germany, this might be my last chance to see Wilno.' Sadly, subsequent developments proved me right.

I went to Wilno on 29 August. The next day I had a conducted tour of the city, and on 31 August I travelled 100 kilometres to Święciany, where I was to meet mother and board the train with her for Warsaw. This meant waiting for several hours at the station, among freshly mobilised recruits from nearby villages. I listened to them talking in their sing-song accents, typical of the eastern regions of Poland. They were going to war without the slightest idea what it meant and were boasting to their wives, mothers and sweethearts: 'You'll see, I swear I'll bring you a watch from Berlin. Not one, several watches . . . a really big clock . . .' It would appear that the stuff of their dreams was timepieces of any description, not motorcars nor jewellery – these did not even exist in their world. Their leaving for the war might thus have been a joyful occasion, were it not for the tearful women, who did not seem to understand – or perhaps they were the ones who understood only too well.

The railway services having been already disrupted, Mother and I were lucky to eventually reach Warsaw. Father, furious, met us at the station. 'Returning to Warsaw was an idiotic move. Didn't I write you as much? I don't need you here.' But it was too late, we were back.

And perhaps just as well. Many of those who stayed behind in Bobrusz, soon to be occupied by the Red Army, were deported deep into the Soviet Union, some to the far north, some to Central Asia.

FOUR

German Invasion, War and Another Partition of Poland

IN WARSAW IT WAS BUSINESS AS USUAL, at least at first sight. In a resounding speech our Foreign Minister, Colonel Beck, rejected the Nazi request for a corridor through Polish territory between Germany and East Prussia: 'There will be no concessions.' Using a border incident staged by Germans dressed in Polish uniform as *casus belli*, the German army invaded Poland at dawn on Friday, 1 September 1939.

I woke that morning to the roar of a low flying silver plane, clearly outlined in the window of my room. A few seconds later an explosion shook the house. For a few moments I failed to connect the two, the plane and the explosion. Then . . . a bomb? The first bomb of my life.

Soon the blast of sirens dispelled any residual doubt. I ran downstairs and into the garden of our block of flats. A few broken windows. Many anxious people milling around. Somehow, I was not frightened. It must have been my lack of imagination. Even later, in much more serious situations, I could never picture myself being hit, lying there bleeding and suffering. Perhaps that was why I didn't panic. My first experience of war didn't shake me unduly, but that single plane was only a paltry foretaste of what was to come.

My father had been moved to the reserves towards the end of 1936, but retained some duties in the Intelligence Department. Now he was recalled to the army but, to his great disappointment, was given the task of organising the Wartime Mail Censorship Bureau. His efforts to get transferred to a field unit were overtaken by events. In the meantime, he managed to get the new Bureau off the ground almost immediately, whatever good that might have done. I was sixteen at the time, and along with Olek Tyrawski, my close friend and contemporary, became a messenger in Father's unit. This, we felt, gave us the right to wear our green, military style school cadet tunics complemented by riding breeches and boots. Self-importantly, we swaggered through the streets of Warsaw in this apparel, on long-since forgotten assignments.

For a few, but only a few, days life seemed fairly normal. On 3 September, the declaration of war by France and Great Britain gave rise to a wave of optimism and joyous demonstrations. Doubts persisted only in the minds of the well informed, and those were few and far between.

Bombs continued to fall. I remember seeing several planes diving onto the Poniatowski bridge but, seen from afar, it was not that impressive. Our anti-aircraft artillery made much noise. During one of the air-raids, my father and I were coming down the street when a fragment of an anti-aircraft shell, having broken a thick branch off a tree, hit the pavement a few metres away. Father didn't bat an eyelid. In the years to come I tried to emulate his example.

Our last few days in Warsaw are but a blur in my memory. As summer ran into autumn, the weather continued to be warm and the sky blue and cloudless. Our forces offered a stubborn and valiant resistance, but when German panzers attacked, we came to understand that a barely modernised Napoleonic army could not defend the country for long against the most modern force of the age. Our army, brave but incomplete and in need of regrouping (at the requests of our allies, 'in order not to provoke the Nazis', our general mobilisation had been delayed for far too long), was facing a German invader long-since on a war footing and helped by the driest of summers.

But such thoughts never entered Olek's and my mind, as we waited impatiently for the call to arms, which seemed to us, in the circumstances, the only worthy aim in life.

My friendship with Olek went back a long way, to the First Form of the *gimnazjum* to be precise. Then, at the age of twelve, Olek was a rather short boy with a large head and big blue eyes. As schoolboys do, we tended to form gangs and mine included Olek, Wacek Koc, Janek Brumer, Jurek Soiński, and a few others. When with his widowed mother, one sister and his older brother, Olek moved to Żolibórz, our own neighbourhood, our friendship grew even closer. We spent a lot of time together, swimming in the Vistula, cycling, canoeing (I had a collapsible rubber canoe, easily packed in two bags). Olek's brother, a veterinary student, was an officer of the reserve, while his older sister, a very bright girl, had just left school. Olek, the youngest of the family, was a boy of great sensitivity, intelligence, decency and integrity.

Barring a few disconnected incidents, I don't recall much of the first week of the war, but I do remember vividly the appeal by the government spokesman, Colonel Umiastowski, broadcast on 6 September. In a grave and solemn voice he appealed to the able male population of Warsaw, threatened by the approaching German army, to leave the city for the east of the country where our forces were regrouping on the Narew-Bug river line.

To this day I don't know who had made this unfortunate decision, but its consequences were deplorable. As in France just over a year later, all roads were soon packed with crowds of refugees. As motorcar ownership was a rarity, the mass of people, whole families, moved either in horse-drawn vehicles of one kind or another or on foot.

The Jewish quarters of the city emptied rapidly. Along with others, these often large Jewish families, now encumbered by their belongings, the men easily recognisable by their typical long black coats and small round caps, were desperately marching out of the city. The moving crowds of refugees were clogging every path east of Warsaw, denying the badly needed roads to the army, often not knowing where they were going or why.

My father's unit, the Mail Censorship Bureau, was also ordered to leave the city. I believe that they had at their disposal several vehicles, some motorised and some horse-drawn, and somewhere on the way Father bought an additional carriage and a pair. About the same time, Olek and I left on bicycles on our way to Garwolin, the town of my childhood, a distance of some sixty kilometres from Warsaw, where we had arranged to meet my parents. As the staff of the Mail Censorship Office included women, there was no problem with including my mother in the evacuation. And so, our entire family left Warsaw to continue the business of war on the line of the River Bug.

Following the same route on our bikes as that taken by most of the refugees, Olek and I witnessed the barbarity of German planes dropping bombs in the midst of the frightened multitude and then machine-gunning the road. The resulting panic was indescribable. Similar sights, repeated later in other parts of the world, have since been described in novels and depicted in films, but for us it was an introduction to the kind of war we had never imagined.

Given the circumstances, the idea of our rendezvous in Garwolin was absurd. Where in Garwolin? We had never specified, but at the time I had no qualms on this score. In the event, on entering the town we stopped by the roadside, sat down on an embankment and, dead tired, awaited the arrival of my parents. We kept scrutinising the crowd, but it was enormous. How we managed to recognise my father's unit, how we did not miss them, will always be a mystery to me. Olek saw them first. Reunited, we decided to escape the crowd and the bombs and continued on our way east, keeping to minor roads.

News we had none. The transistor radio was not invented until many years later. We could only assume that the situation in the country both generally and locally was changing from one minute to the next. Our intention was to cross the River Bug and there join the army 'reorganising for the purpose of recovering the lost territories'. Even the adults agreed with us that losing the war was inconceivable. Defeat could not even be considered.

Isolated images from our wanderings are forever imprinted on my memory: pictures of villages burned to the ground with brick chimneys alone standing among the ashes, the sickening smell of burnt animal flesh, the distant glow of blazing homesteads, nights spent in moving carts in that no man's land between wakefulness and light sleep, between reality and dream. Thus, half-asleep, we had to keep an eye on the road to avoid running into other refugees.

In one of the villages Olek and I went in search of food when suddenly a German plane came overhead. The village seemed deserted. We were alone in the market place, sticking out like two sore thumbs. The plane dived and strafed the square. We saw bullets hitting the ground in front of us and behind us, but they didn't touch us. It was all over in seconds. To tell the truth, there hadn't even been enough time to get scared.

At long last we arrived at the banks of the River Bug. The other side was supposed to be the last line of Polish resistance. Another section of my father's unit also achieved the prearranged rallying point, but their journey was futile: there was no mail in circulation. The rapid turn of events precluded any contact between individual units.

We crossed the River Bug without much difficulty. We felt reasonably safe. Suddenly, someone shouted a warning about approaching German tanks. I couldn't see them. And then, within seconds, there was the mounted figure of my father galloping ahead. 'I'll see for myself!' he shouted. I had no idea how and where he managed to procure the horse. Anyway, we had no weapons and we could escape only by running back towards the river. As we did so, the tanks appeared just behind us. One of them opened fire. 'Take cover there,' calmly ordered Father, now dismounted, pointing to the steep river bank. We ran, while he, in his officer uniform, leisurely strolled, as if on a country walk, seemingly unperturbed by the machine gun fire coming in short bursts.

I turned back. 'Hurry up Dad . . . please hurry up!' I pleaded with him, only to be sharply rebuked. The next moment, we were all hiding at the water's edge, flat against the slope of the two-metre-high bank, clinging to the dry grass. But it was not a safe hiding place. A German tank turned the curve of the river and aimed its machine gun straight at us. Wedged between the steep bank and the river, we were surrounded. Soldiers on foot approached our hiding place with their rifles at the ready and motioned us to climb the bank. Father was in uniform, Olek and I wore our school cadet tunics, all the others were in civvies. We were prisoners. I expected to be shot there and then. I wanted to express my despondency, but my knowledge of German was not up to the task. 'How do you say "shoot"?' I asked Father.

'*Schiessen*,' he answered. With all the gravity at my command, I turned to the nearest soldier: '*Bitte schiessen*.'

'*Nein, nein*,' he shook his head as he lowered the rifle. Thinking about it now, it must have been quite a tragi-comical scene.

They marched us to a school building already holding other detainees, several wounded among them. Father found the German commander and, helped by his fluent German, soon established some kind of contact with him. The man was polite and their conversation very urbane, even amicable. The officer had no intention of keeping us. 'We are the *Wehrmacht*, the army,' he said, 'and I'll let you go, but beware of the Gestapo who follow close behind us.'

My first encounter with the German army was coming to an end. Just before we left, one of the soldiers took me aside. 'Are you a soldier?' he asked. With my index finger I traced a little circle on my forehead, a gesture full of meaning even for Germans. 'Are you calling a German soldier crazy?' he shouted, furious. Luckily one of his fellows calmed him down, 'Leave him alone. We did not want this war any more than they did. It's the damned governments . . .'

Until 1944, this was probably my longest face-to-face encounter with German soldiers. Subsequently, our exchanges would be restricted to: '*Hände hoch*!' and perhaps a few other invectives and sharp commands during the frequent searches of suspects stopped in the streets of Warsaw.

Once released, we took stock of the situation. It was desperate. The Germans were obviously already east of the River Bug, which was supposed to be the last line of the Polish defence. We decided to cross back to the west side, where perhaps we could still find some operational Polish units. As far as we knew, Warsaw was still fighting. Could our forces be regrouping in order to relieve the capital? We waded through the river on 17 September, a hot summer's day, more like the middle of August. The sky was cloudless.

Suddenly, an agitated and frightened man ran up to my father: 'The Russians have crossed the border and seem to be welcomed by the Germans.'

The man was given no credence. 'Nonsense!' 'Impossible!' 'A bloody lie.' 'We don't need defeatists!' came the shouts from all sides.

I'll leave out the details of our subsequent wanderings. Eventually, we did manage to locate an operational Polish unit and Father went to offer his services, as well as the services of all those of us who were fit to fight. He returned utterly despondent. There was no organised resistance, no ammunition and no orders. In short, we had to face reality. We were defeated. The Red Army was indeed taking over the eastern provinces of the country with German acquiescence. The worst possible scenario was unfolding before our eyes. For the fourth time in her history Poland was being partitioned, this time between Hitler and Stalin.

Father decided to return to Warsaw, either to take part in the continuing defence of the besieged city or as a stepping stone to a further journey; I am not sure whether the idea of joining the Polish Army in exile arose then or later. The subsequent events proved him right, inasmuch as refugees who fell into Russian hands were systematically deported into the depths of the Soviet Union, while officers were arrested and sent to camps. Not many survived. Some 5,000 had been murdered by the NKVD, the precursor of KGB, in Katyń. A further 25,000 were shot later on Stalin's and Beria's orders. Only recently, in 1993, a warrant to this effect signed by Stalin, Gromyko, Mikoyan and the rest of the Soviet Politburo has come to light in the archives of NKVD.

FIVE

Warsaw Under Occupation.
The Arrest of my Father

WE RETURNED TO WARSAW TOO LATE TO FIGHT. After its valiant defence, the capital had surrendered on 27 September. From the perspective of 1939 the extent of the destruction had seemed terrible. But our framework of reference could not encompass the barbarities yet to come, and what we saw was just a foretaste of the tragic fate the city was to suffer several years hence. However, Żolibórz had largely been spared and our house stood intact. Jasia, our maid who had stayed behind in the flat, did not expect us back so soon and had stored most of our belongings at Mrs Tyrawska's. Father was adamant, 'It would be madness to return home. The Germans are bound to find me there and arrest me.' In spite of Mother's protestations we went to stay in Konstancin, at Mrs Strasburger's, next door to our old villa, which was by now in the hands of new owners.

Father decided to try and get to France, where the new Polish Army was being formed. I was to accompany him. But to undertake the journey we needed false papers, such as passports of a neutral country. And so Father went to meet the honorary consul of Peru, a man he had known previously through his brother, who had held that office himself for several years.

Events of the two or three weeks following our return home are no longer clear in my memory. I do remember an elderly lady of our acquaintance who kept angrily reproaching my father, me, and many others for having supported the regime now disintegrating so pitifully around us. But the defeat of Poland was a blow to all of us and to me, personally: my world had collapsed like a house of cards.

Little by little we were finding out about the fate of our friends. Roman Mularczyk was back. Taken by the Russians, he had succeeded in convincing his captors that his white hands, far from being the evidence of his gentlemanly origins, were due to recent surgery. This was in fact true. In August 1939, having passed his final secondary school examinations, he was conscripted into the compulsory youth service to build fortifications on the Soviet border, a detail he did not divulge to the Russians. Heavy physical work, mainly manual digging, produced blisters on his hands. These got infected and eventually needed surgery. He thus convinced the Bolsheviks of his truly proletarian status.

I awaited our departure for France with great impatience. In the beginning of October, we were planning to leave at the first opportunity. We even went to Warsaw to buy a few items necessary for the journey. Then, on 20 October, Father went to the capital again, while we stayed behind in Konstancin. About 3 p.m. a car stopped in front of the house. Two uniformed Germans entered. Their peaked caps bore the letters SD (*Sicherheit Dienst* or Security Service) and a skull with crossbones.

'Where is Captain Likiernik?'

'In Warsaw.'

'Is he coming back?'

'Yes.'

'Then we shall wait for him.'

They sat down, but neither we nor they had yet learned how one was to behave in these circumstances. Through laxity which later would be unthinkable, they did not stop me leaving the room. I contrived to send a messenger to Jeziorna station where Father would be arriving on the Warsaw–Konstancin narrow gauge train, warning him not to return home. Back in the room I told the two Germans that Father would soon be arriving at the Konstancin station, where in reality he never alighted. At around 6 p.m. the Gestapo men left for the station, taking me with them so that I would point Father out to them. I managed to hide my anxiety. They stopped a number of men resembling Father but did not, of course, find him.

After the penultimate train we returned home. Father would never have left it so late. I was confident of success, when suddenly the doors opened and there was Father, pointedly saying to Mother, 'Now you see who was right.' And then, 'Gentlemen, I am at your disposal,' and to me 'Get me my winter coat.' He kissed Mother and me. The two Germans took him by the arms, one on each side, and they left.

Later I found out that my messenger, an inexperienced lad, didn't bother to wait for the last train. Father, seeing the car at our gate, guessed that the Gestapo were waiting for him. He went round the back of the house hoping to find the maid. She was working in the stable. 'Yes, they are here looking for you,' she said.

'I'll go into hiding,' decided Father.

But the maid warned him, 'They've threatened to take the mistress and master Staś instead.'

'Oh, in that case . . .' and he went inside.

The next day, without telling Mother, I went to Warsaw, directly to the Gestapo headquarters in Aleja Szucha; the kind of act soon to be recognised as most unwise. I climbed the enormous staircase. 'What do you want?' brusquely asked the SS man on guard.

'My father was arrested yesterday. I would like to find out his whereabouts.'

'*Raus!*' he screamed, grabbing my shoulder, and kicked me down the stairs.

Mother retraced my steps later in the day, taking with her Father's toothbrush, soap and a towel. She received a polite reply: 'He doesn't need anything now.' It sounded ominous. And then there was a long silence. No information for months.

As the worst seemed to have already happened, we decided to return to Żolibórz. Though the window panes were gone, the flat seemed habitable. Glass was scarce and for the time being we had to do with plywood. We recovered our possessions and started some kind of new life. The Polish currency, the złoty, was still in circulation and we had enough money to begin with. The Germans had not quite settled in as yet; they needed time to organise their murderous system of oppression. Meanwhile they were even distributing free soup in the poorer quarters of Warsaw. However, posters carrying orders had already begun to appear all round the city:

1. All schools for children over the age of twelve are to be closed until further notice.
(The spurious reasoning for this was the risk of typhus. This 'temporary' order was to remain in force until 1945.)
2. Under the penalty of death, all radio receivers are to be handed in to the police within three days.

This order was unexpected, but there was no way of evading it. I damaged whatever I could inside our brand new modern American radio, I removed and crushed the valves and took the useless ebonite box to the police station. That was the first and only time that I had obeyed a German order other than under immediate threat. An hour later, the radio salesman from our local shop appeared on our doorstep. He suggested that he could exchange the radio we recently bought from him for an old model and then hide our modern receiver. Were these the first shoots of an underground activity?

❧

Everyday life was becoming difficult. The RGO, The Polish Social Assistance Organisation, came legally into being and started issuing work certificates. They were quite generous and I easily obtained one of them, even though they were of little use. It was important to lay one's hands on a document certifying that one performed a job of value to the Germans and to carry it on one's person at all times. RGO also ran soup kitchens. These became quite popular and though one may not have eaten well there, it was always in very good company.

Christmas 1939 in Warsaw was not a happy time. But France and Great Britain were on our side, and we kept hoping for an imminent offensive against Germany in the west. But it was not to be. What has become known as *la drôle de guerre*, or the phoney war, was not at all phoney for us and we had no means of knowing what it was like elsewhere. My friends and I were busy preparing for an illegal crossing into Hungary and Yugoslavia and hence to France, to join the army being organised there – as we heard on the grapevine – by Gen. Sikorski. Our intention was to travel together: Janek Brumer, Jurek Soiński, Wacek Koc, Olek Tyrawski and I. Janek's uncle promised to provide us with a few gold dollar pieces, needed to set up the escape. Our excitement reached its peak when Janek reported that he had established the necessary contacts and that we would be on our way the following week.

One day Roman Mularczyk came to see me. He was sceptical. We all entertained some doubts as to the reliability of Janek's contacts. We were aware of his gullibility, which was combined with a foolhardy enthusiasm. Roman raised a number of points:

- Was the chain of contacts truly reliable?
- Why go to France? There was enough scope for action here.
- Let a small group go first and once they succeeded, the rest of us would follow.

He convinced me.

Soiński and Brumer left Warsaw. We did not hear from them for a long time – but when we finally did it was from Oświęcim, or Auschwitz. The camp, destined soon to become notorious, was under construction. My friends were among its first slave labour builders.

Eventually, Brumer was released and two years later in Warsaw he related to us the details of the venture. The group had assembled in Zakopane, in the Tatra mountains, the intended starting point for crossing the frontier on skis. However, the operation must have been either organised by the Germans themselves or with their connivance, as at dawn of the day of their departure the group were arrested. After several months in Auschwitz, Soiński contracted typhus and died. His parents received a cable to that effect.

Soon after relating the story to us, Brumer was rearrested and sent back to the camp. As a camp veteran, identifiable by the low number tattooed on his arm, he was treated with relative leniency – this was some quirk in the mentality of the Gestapo – and survived the war, but eventually I lost touch with him.

Roman's advice, then, had probably saved the lives of Olek Tyrawski, Wacek Koc and myself.

Throughout this time there was no news of Father. One day, on the advice of a friend, armed with a photograph and some favourite object of his, Mother went to consult a clairvoyant. I took it as a joke, but in reality it was not a laughing matter. After all, neither I nor anybody else could offer any better advice. The clairvoyant started telling my mother something about Father's escape to the east, and then suddenly changed her mind: he was alive and on his way west, now somewhere on the pre-war Polish-German border.

Was it true? We had no means of checking. But it rekindled our hope. A month later a stranger knocked on our door. We didn't know him from Adam, but he showed us Father's initials, TL, drawn in his notebook in his own unique style. He told us that soon after his arrest Father had been transferred to a small concentration camp in Schneidemühl, or Piła in Polish, a town on the old frontier. Taken to the camp in October, he remained there for a month. All the prisoners had been put to work but, considering it a violation of his officer status, he refused to comply. He became known among his fellow prisoners for the way he kept up their morale by entertaining them with amusing stories and anecdotes. He refused to eat the camp fare and inmates going out to work would bring him food from outside, knowing that they risked flogging if discovered.

Once, when a guard addressed him by the pronoun *du*, i.e. in the familiar second person singular, he put him in his place in no uncertain terms. This act of defiance could have ended in tragedy. As the guard made to hit him, Father wrenched out the heavy cast iron gate of the tiled stove and threatened the SS man. The guard refrained from shooting him dead on the spot only because Father was a prisoner in transit. As we learned much later, he was about to be moved first to Polizei Presidium Alexanderplatz in Berlin, and then to the notorious Moabit prison, also in that city.

A few weeks later, some time in November, news reached us that Father was still alive, but otherwise the only reliable information we had of him for a long time had been that brought by the stranger.

I had always been very attached to my father and his incarceration by the enemy invested him in my eyes with the aura of a hero. At the time I was still a believer, and I prayed for him regularly. In fact, I did much more than that. At sixteen, I was beginning to learn about sex. Our maid, Jasia, a pretty girl, was quite willing to proceed with my education but after Father's arrest, in order not to weaken the power of my prayers, I gave up my apprenticeship. I am pretty sure that Father, had he known about it, would have advised me against this way of securing his release. However, I had to use all methods at my disposal.

At about this time one of my Father's friends, who ran a small metallurgical workshop, offered me a job and I accepted. This was my first experience of gainful employment. Several machines were housed in a kind of barrack where we were busy making padlocks. On the first day I was oiling pieces of sheet metal and passing them to the man working the press. On the second day, I was asked to support the end of a metal rod while it was being bent and cut to make the padlock hoops. But later, when I was wanted elsewhere, my 'job' was taken over by a wooden stool. This was a rude shock to my self-esteem, and greatly affected my ambitions in the discipline of metallurgy. The following Sunday I discussed the affront with Roman in Konstancin and withdrew my services.

Some time in late October or early November it became clear that the secondary schools would not reopen – after all, in Hitler's grand plan all Slav peoples were to be reduced to serfdom – and that was when clandestine teaching first began. This was an enormous undertaking, hardly since recognised outside Poland. Actually, the tradition of clandestine education, such as the illegal teaching of the Polish language under the tsarist rule, had persisted through the time of partitions and was still very much alive and ready to be rekindled when the need arose. Clandestine schools therefore came into existence in an almost natural way. We simply returned to the educational methods familiar to teachers, parents and young people alike, and stepped into the still-warm shoes of the preceding generation. The occupying power meanwhile left us in no doubt that any unauthorised gathering of young people would lead to their immediate deportation to concentration camps.

The underground classes of about five students each were held in private flats and people would filter in singly at fifteen minute intervals. The class would thus assemble over a period of about an hour, starting at 8 a.m. The teacher would arrive last and, having given his or her lesson, would depart to hold a class elsewhere. Another one would come half an hour later and so on. In my class we were all about sixteen years old, holders of the junior matriculation certificate of general education. To be able to sit exams for the matriculation certificate proper we needed two more years of the specialised secondary school course called *Liceum*, in either the humanities, mathematics, or science.

Under the circumstances, our teachers acquired entirely new personae. Enclosed with groups of just five of us in small private rooms, they seemed to have become human. For instance, Mr Kociejowski had never been able to cope with a form of some forty 'monsters' before the war. Now we discovered that he was a well-educated and exceedingly well-informed man who could talk with great eloquence, even passion, about Darwin, Lamarc, etc. Even my relationship with Mme Klimaszewska, our French teacher, had greatly improved. And the process of learning became for us a kind of patriotic duty – forbidden, and so an act of defiance. We were gaining an education not so much for ourselves as against the Germans.

Not many details of that first year of the occupation remain in my mind. The winter passed in organising the underground classes, gathering news, trying to get in touch with people who would lead us, who would tell us what to do. There were rumours of an Underground Army being organised by officers, about weapons that had been hidden by Polish forces at the end of hostilities in 1939. But as yet we saw no chance of any real action.

SIX

The Dawn of the Underground.
The Onset of Persecution

THE EVIL ODOUR OF ANTI-SEMITISM ENTERED WARSAW in the wake of the German army. Within days the first anti-Jewish orders were posted on the walls and poster pillars of the capital. Naturally, Mother and I ignored them. However, we were warned by the house administration that the books had been checked and that a mark had been made against our name, no doubt for further attention. Would we be thrown out into the street? Mother contacted the chief administrator, a socialist of the old school who had known Father from the time of the anti-tsarist revolution of 1905. The compromising marks were erased. This was the first of a series of miracles which allowed us to go on as if nothing, or almost nothing, had happened.

Life was difficult for all, but we had an additional handicap. We refused to wear the armbands obligatory for anybody unable to boast of four Aryan grandparents. We simply ignored the obscene Nazi Nuremberg laws. Our Slavic appearance made it possible, but the risk was always there, especially as our family, long-established in Warsaw, was well known.

The family of Father's sister, Aunt Alina Wojecka, her husband, their daughter, Marie, a linguist, and their son Stanisław, a final year medical student, took a similar risk by meeting the German iniquities with the same contempt. Their youngest son, Piotr, was away somewhere in the east. My Mother's relatives, however, lived in that quarter of Warsaw which was destined to become the infamous Warsaw ghetto. But for the time being until the wall went up we remained in touch with them.

My friend Wacek Koc, whose parents were divorced, had hitherto lived with his father, a colonel of the Polish Army. At the start of the war his father fell into Soviet hands and as an 'enemy of the people' disappeared into the prison camps of the USSR. His mother, Mrs Koc, lived with her daughter Jaga and her other son Andrzej in Żolibórz, in a villa not far from us. When Wacek joined them, their villa became my second home. Wacek and I had become friends in secondary school but now, as neighbours, we spent more and more time in each other's company. In years to come the Koc family would play an important part in my life and I'll have a lot to say about them later.

Mrs Koc taught Polish literature at the Emilia Plater *gimnazjum* for girls. She was not only an attractive and charming lady but also a very well educated and highly cultured one. Her students adored her and Wacek was not loath to profit from the associated advantages. The Koc family had a great patriotic tradition. Both his father, Colonel Leon Koc, and his father's brother, Adam, a politician and a minister in the Polish government, had spent their youth fighting with the Piłsudski Legion, the veterans of which had an important role in rebuilding the country. Wacek, therefore, had good connections and was well placed to seek contacts with the Underground.

In the spring of 1940 Wacek got in touch with his cousin Edmund Gurda, Mundek for short. Mundek, a married man with a small daughter, a PT teacher and a lieutenant of the reserve, was involved with counter-espionage. In the early months of the German occupation Mundek started organising an intelligence network and needed young helpers. I didn't know anything about it until Wacek introduced us. Mundek was our first serious contact. I was seventeen years old.

Some time before that, Olek Tyrawski and I had attended a clandestine meeting. We expected a lecture on bomb making, on the use of weapons, or perhaps on tactical aspects of a guerrilla war. Instead we had been treated to a eulogy of a certain Salazar, apparently a model head of state. Unwittingly, we had allowed ourselves to be enticed to an ultra-nationalist meeting. In spite of our political naivety we soon spotted the irrelevance of the lecture to our desire to handle weapons and fight. Salazar and his neutral country might have been several light years away as far as we were concerned.

Mundek was in another league altogether. He was about thirty years old, broad of shoulder, muscular, strong, and certainly not a politician. I shall never forget our first assignment. It concerned a certain Mr X, who was wanted by the Underground; he had

apparently been wounded and his trail had gone cold. He lived near
the Marymont tramway terminus and our job was to find out
whether he had returned to the vicinity of his home. This meant
keeping the street under surveillance. We reached the terminus at
about 7 a.m. and found a suitable place from which we could,
unobserved, watch the area. At 2 p.m. we were still there, having
seen nothing of interest. However, being new to the game, we were
under the false impression that we were indeed invisible.
Fortunately, the Germans too were as yet inexperienced and there
were no consequences. We had successfully carried out our
assignment, boring though it had been.

At the time, Mundek was looking for accommodation and
Mother, without asking for details, let him a room in our flat. One
day as Mundek was entertaining a man, a stranger to me, in his
room, familiar metallic clicking sounds reached me above their
voices. I recognised their source at once. Before the war I had often
dismantled and cleaned Father's pistol and the clicks coming from
next door were unmistakably the same. Intrigued and eager, I was
on the point of going to ask, when a thought stopped me in my
tracks. Wouldn't it run counter to the rules of the Underground?
Eventually, I managed to get Mundek to invite me into his sanctuary
as he was busy cleaning and oiling the weapons dug out somewhere
from a secret cache. Little by little, he began to trust me.

One day Mundek sent me to an address in Żolibórz, our suburb,
to collect for him a suitcase containing weapons. I pressed the bell
as instructed: two short, one long. An attractive young woman,
Mundek's wife as I would later learn, opened the door. I gave her the
password and was handed a small yet heavy suitcase. After a
moment's hesitation she added a revolver. 'Do you know how to use
it?' she asked me as an afterthought, about to close the door.

What answer could a lad of seventeen give to an attractive
woman? 'Yes, of course, nothing to it.' Could I possibly admit never
having used a pistol of this type before? I pushed the revolver into
my belt – I did not have a belly in those days – and thus armed I
turned back to the Żeromski Park, the quickest way home.

I had not yet reached the park when I came face to face with a
policeman in navy-blue uniform. These men, popularly referred to
as 'the blues', were members of the old Polish police force, now
performing police duties under the occupying power. I was about to
pass him calmly, when he raised his arm and called sharply: 'A
moment, young man!'

'What do you want?' I retorted with equal brusqueness.

'Open the suitcase.'

I knew that the weapons would be wrapped in layers of greasy paper. I took the risk and opened it. The cop pushed his finger inside, felt the paper.

'Come with me!' he barked.

'Where to?'

'The police station.'

It was a longish walk. He was on his own.

'We shall see,' I said to myself. I had the revolver. It was loaded. As we walked steadily side by side, the man engaged me in conversation.

'What's the stuff in your suitcase?'

'Have a guess.'

What had his exploring finger told him? I wondered. We continued on our way for several minutes before he ventured: 'Is it saccharine?'

The artificial sweetener, so precious in the absence of sugar, was always in short supply. Me, a black marketeer? I stopped and faced him. I assumed that the safety-catch was off and that I would be the first on the draw; both suppositions that I would never verify. I looked him straight in the eye and said slowly, forcing each word through my teeth, 'My good man, I would not advise you to sweeten your tea with my saccharine . . .' I left the sentence hanging in the air.

Suddenly disconcerted, flustered, he looked at me, 'What do you mean? You are a funny one.' Then he understood. 'All right, all right, you can give me a sweetener and go.'

I doubt that he meant the double entendre. But he had certainly understood me. I only had twenty złotys on me, virtually nothing, but he took the banknote and turned to go. He seemed greatly relieved; we both were.

Back home, I kept mum about it. I did not want Mundek to have doubts about my ability to carry out similar assignments in the future. At last I was doing what I had been wishing for. If not using them as yet, I was helping to get the weapons ready.

Soon after, Olek and I were formally admitted to ZWZ, the Armed Combat Association or the Underground Army, which owed allegiance to the Polish Government in Exile, in London. We were sworn in by Mundek and another man, Alexander, whom I did not know at the time, but whom I would meet again later in much less propitious circumstances.

Due to Mundek, our flat became a meeting place, a safe house for the conspirators, in brief a *melina*, Polish slang for a haunt of villains. But I was happy. At last I had a chance to do something.

Some time before we had received a letter from a Berlin lawyer, Mr Paul Szczygiel. He requested proof that my father's active army service had been terminated before the start of the war. That was the first indirect but official confirmation that Father was alive. Post-haste we found the necessary documents and sent them to the lawyer. Again nothing happened. And then one day, as mother was tidying up the flat, the door bell rang, followed by loud knocking. Two men were standing on our doorstep, one in the Gestapo uniform which I knew so well from the time of Father's arrest, the other a civilian but in the typical mackintosh of a plainclothes policeman. '*Das ist der Sohn*,' said the Gestapo man as he pushed me out of the way and entered the dining room.

'Where is your mother?' he asked. She heard him and came into the room.

'This is the end,' I thought to myself. She must have reached the same conclusion.

'Frau Likiernik?' asked the Gestapo man. 'I am here on behalf of your husband,' he continued. 'He is in my charge, in Moabit, and he needs money. Do you understand? You give me złotys and I'll give him marks.' A kind of a drawing-room conversation followed. 'Your husband refuses to eat prison fare and I have to get his food outside. This is not easy – he fancies sweet things.' He stopped for a moment and then looked at me sternly, '*Keine Dumheiten machen*, don't fool around, young man. Do you understand? Father's orders.'

I understood only too well. 'Fooling around . . .? I have no time to waste on stupidities,' I said with amazement. 'I have to work hard to provide for my mother.'

That was the end of the unexpected visit. After the war we would learn that Father did receive the money. He had a special knack of getting on with people, and with his fluent German he even managed to tame one of his guards.

In the early stages of the German occupation the persecution of Poles and of Polish Jews was sporadic, only just beginning. The heel of the jackboot was coming down in slow motion, deliberately and, I suppose, in accordance with a pre-determined plan. The first aim was to impose obedience. Each new order, not very dramatic in itself, prepared ground for the next one. People were being randomly arrested. Only accidentally would we learn that this individual, or another, usually a lawyer or a doctor, was in prison, or had just disappeared, destination unknown. But on the whole the repression seemed to have been individually targeted.

Mass expropriation of Poles in Poznań and generally in western Poland, which had been incorporated into the Reich, started in mid-winter. Entire families were thrown on to the streets and expelled to the *General Government*, the zone of Poland ruled by the German Governor General Frank, who made his residence in Wawel, the Royal Palace in Cracow.

The Nazi beast was starting to bare its fangs, but we could not even begin to imagine the enormity of the atrocities still to come.

One positive bit of news which spread around Warsaw that winter was that of the reopening of three technical vocational schools. These schools would issue diplomas in railway engineering, chemistry and ceramic engineering. I enrolled into the chemistry course. Many of my friends and school fellows did the same, among them Olek Tyrawski and Zbyszek Przestępski. However the proposed opening day, 19 September 1940, became memorable, but for a very different reason.

That day I got up earlier than usual and was just leaving for school when an unusual spectacle stopped me. Soldiers in the street! What was happening? There were as yet few people about, but soldiers were posted about every hundred metres and would not let anyone leave the street or even cross to the other side. Strange . . . Then we saw lorries filled to capacity with men, all civilians, speeding down the street. Mother had a quick look out and said 'Close the door.'

'They must be moving prisoners from one prison to another,' I said.

'You may be right,' Mother mused, 'But so many of them?'

That was true, there were too many lorries, but what to do next? I was in a quandary.

Eventually, I decided to ignore the soldiers and the lorries and to leave for school as if nothing had happened. I was walking towards the tram stop at Inwalidów Square when a shout of '*Hände hoch!*' suddenly stopped me in my tracks. A quick body search and I was directed on to the Square, where dozens of men were sitting on the grass in small groups surrounded by guards with rifles at the ready. We waited and waited. People occasionally exchanged a few words in undertones. All of a sudden we were mustered into a column of threes and marched to Wilson Square. Passing under the windows of our block of flats I took off my hat and waved it about. Our neighbour, Mrs Hetlinger, the wife of a lawyer and now a POW in Germany, noticed me from her usual post by the window and left, presumably to call my mother. My gesture caused some merriment among the guards.

In the Square, still in threes, we were told to form queues to the lorries. Sudden rifle shots . . . a young boy was trying to escape, he was hit, fell down. Several girls – it was not their turn this time – approached the lorries and looked at people's faces, perhaps to pass the news to their families. We had no idea what it was all about.

My turn came. The German examined my certificate, issued by the Polish Social Assistance Organisation, returned it to me and pointed to the bench on a still largely empty lorry. The operation continued. Suddenly, an officer pointed to the boy sitting next to me. 'Your papers!' He examined them. '*Raus*!' he screamed. He whispered something to the guard. I vaguely understood – the age of sixteen was being mentioned. I was seventeen. I wanted out, so badly. I tried my bad German: 'So am I . . .'

My neighbour on the other side came to my assistance. 'He is seventeen.' His German was infinitely better than mine.

'Your papers.' Impatiently, the officer clicked his fingers. He examined my certificate. 'We start at eighteen,' he said to the soldier standing next to him. '*Wracaj do domu*, go home,' said the soldier in Silesian-accented Polish.

Another instance of my devil's luck, the luck of the devil. Or I'd like to think so. I looked back at the people in the lorry. There but for the grace of God . . . That morning the Germans rounded up all men from the age of fifteen to sixty in our district. They searched all the flats, including ours. They took boys of my age and even younger. Perhaps the officer who let me go had made a mistake. Perhaps it was only in his eyes that one had to be eighteen to be culpable. I would hear later that on that day alone about 30,000 men had been taken to Auschwitz. The camp was now ready and could not be allowed to stand half empty. After about three months cables would start arriving: 'Your husband, your son, has died.' The spurious cause of death was usually given as typhus.

I was now longing to do something, to fight back in whatever way I could. Anything was better than being trampled upon like this. The resolve not to die like a rabbit torn to pieces by wolves became irresistible. The humiliation of being defenceless, of being rounded up like so many heads of cattle, was unendurable.

The day after the roundup I went back to school. It was supposed to be a vocational school, as only these were allowed by the authorities, but it was run on good old secondary school principles. We had excellent teachers. As the universities and all teaching establishments of higher learning remained closed, some of our teachers were, in fact, university professors or lecturers. I made new friends, among them Zygmunt Brzosko and his fiancée, Zosia Laskowska. Their names are fresh in my mind as I have recently, in my old age, visited their graves in the Powązki cemetery in Warsaw. Zygmunt excelled in everything, from gym to maths. Zosia, willowy and blonde, to her great regret taller than Zygmunt, was charming and vivacious. She was studying medicine at the clandestine university, combining it with conspiratorial work in the AK, the Home Army. In order to make a living she volunteered to be a louse-feeder; she carried a box of these blood-sucking parasites attached to her thigh. The lice were required for the production of the typhus vaccine for the German forces; the volunteer hosts were quite well paid, but the constant itching was unbearable. When I met them in 1940, Zygmunt and Zosia had only four more years to live, and what a life! Now, in my sunset years, as I am writing my memoirs, I can but think of them as my children: indeed my own children are older now than these friends were on the day of their death.

SEVEN

The Hard Days of Occupation

FROM THE DISTANCE OF MORE THAN HALF A CENTURY, the true duration of the war is difficult to fathom. Only six years, but what years! Never-ending, every one lasting an eternity. I cannot even begin to order the events in any meaningful way. Individual, more or less significant, episodes come to my mind, but their temporal connections are lost. If only I had kept a diary. But no, even that wouldn't have been an answer; it would have vanished, like the rest of my belongings, every single one of them.

I think it is only now that I am beginning to make sense of it all. Grey days followed one another, only to disappear into a kind of no man's land between personally significant episodes and the much more weighty happenings affecting all, some of us more then others. Today one can just see the tip of the iceberg, but the rest has been lost in the sea of oblivion. Each hour could have been your last, yet it need not have automatically become memorable.

Olek and I were back at school together, now keen to attend and eager to learn. In addition, Mundek enrolled us in the officers' school of the Underground Army. These classes were also held in groups of five, in the flat of each student in turn. Our instructor was a cavalry captain whom we only knew as Junosza, his *nom de guerre*. The course kept very close to the pre-war officers' school curriculum. We even built a kind of war games table for exercises, though ours was made of sand in the cellar of Zygmunt Zabierzowski, the trainer-to-be of the Cuban athletic team, victorious at the Montreal Olympics, who has since died. We would also hold field exercises such as planning of defence operations, terrain orientation in nearby woods and similar places. Our instructor, a relatively young man, had an aristocratic bearing and must have looked smart in uniform. Unfortunately his generation of officers lacked that general cultural background of their predecessors, my father's generation.

Megalomaniac theories such as 'Why should we learn foreign languages, let the others learn Polish,' were sad to hear. Also, in the middle of the war, the relevance of such subjects as *Kodeks Honorowy*, The Code of Honour, was, to say the least, questionable. We had to learn the principles of arbitration in affairs of honour and the rules of duelling. We were left in no doubt, for instance, that in a duel with pistols, raising the collar of one's jacket to cover the whiteness of one's shirt was totally unacceptable. At times it was difficult to keep a straight face. After so thorough a grounding in the principles and practice of warfare, we were now supposed to be fully prepared to meet the Nazis head on.

Also about that time, Mundek confided in my mother that he knew he was being followed. 'This time I managed to shake them off, but I'd better move out,' were his words. He was right. Two or three days later, as he reached a supposedly safe house for a prearranged meeting, the Germans were there waiting for him. Having realised that he was walking into an ambush, he rushed downstairs and would have got away had not the soldiers asked a little boy 'Which way did the thief run?' and he, not knowing any better, pointed the way. These were the early stages of the occupation. Later nobody ever saw anything, even small children had learned the lesson. The Germans caught up with Mundek and shot him on the spot. He left a wife and a small daughter.

But I have outrun the course of events. Spring 1940 was, in fact, memorable. Totally unaware of the phoney nature of the war in the west, always in awe of the combined power of France and Great Britain, we fully expected an allied offensive. Whenever *Gadzinówka*, or 'Vermin News', as we contemptuously called the German-published Polish language newspaper, brought news bad from our point of view, it was as a rule ascribed to propaganda. And so the successes of the German Army in Belgium, Holland and France had been met with the usual disbelief. But as the news became more persistent, Warsaw was staggered. Deprived of radios, we could not check by listening to foreign broadcasts. The clandestine press was still in its early, tentative stages. When the extent of the disaster became clear – Dunkirk, the fall of Paris, the armistice – there was no more room for doubt.

I remember the time well. Roman Mularczyk and I were in my flat, deep in doom and gloom.

'Now that France has fallen, we are lost . . .'

'How could they allow this to happen? They knew what had happened to us. They had all the details of the September blitz. Weren't they supposed to be much more powerful than Poland?'

The world was disintegrating around us. We were in despair. But deep down, I am sure of it even now, I didn't believe that this was the end. The feeling was not based on rational thinking. There was proof enough that our defeat was final . . . but was it? I couldn't accept it. I rejected the awful truth. It did not even cross my mind that England would be able to go on fighting on her own, when France, our ally and the country of Napoleon – idolised by so many Poles – had collapsed just like a house of cards. Perhaps the USA . . . That day was among the most depressing, the most difficult days I had known. Suddenly, the might of the Nazi state loomed larger than ever.

I don't know when or how we learned of the continued valiant resistance of the British. The bombing of England was widely reported in the Gadzinówka. Muffled echoes of the Battle of Britain were reaching Warsaw. My admiration for Great Britain and for Winston Churchill grew apace. Without them, we would have certainly been lost. We had never heard of General de Gaulle. But we did learn of the arrival in London of General Sikorski, and of the Polish Government in Exile.

At the same time, the strength of the Polish Underground was steadily increasing but, in spite of the age-long tradition of clandestine work, mistakes were being made again and again. I'll never forget the look of amazement on Mundek's face when our other tenant, Mrs Szwed, the wife of a colonel, a prisoner-of-war, averred one day: 'I know that General Rowecki is the head of the Underground.' Shortly after, the general was arrested and shot. I don't suspect our charming tenant to have been implicated in the affair, but Mrs Szwed's knowledge of his identity has always remained a mystery to me.

In addition to the officer training, our underground activity involved the distribution of *Biuletyn Informacyjny*, a newsletter of the Underground Army, and the collection of intelligence regarding the movements of German army units. One of the informers included in my rounds was a Mr Artysiewicz, whose name, of course, I didn't learn until much later. He was about fifty years old and lived with his wife very modestly in a bedsitter in Powązki, a quarter of Warsaw. He used to be an NCO in the Polish army, and was a gunsmith, now working for the Germans, repairing small arms in the nearby barracks. He thus had access to weapons, and also to important intelligence. In September 1939 the Germans had killed his only son, aged eighteen, and now an irrepressible desire for vengeance seemed to fill his entire life. Every day after work, under the noses of the guards and in spite of regular searches, this man would bring out of the barracks ammunition, complete revolvers and spare parts. The risk was constant and absolute. As there was always a ready market for weapons, he could have profited handsomely from the contraband by selling some, even if only occasionally. He and his wife lived in poverty, on a diet of potatoes and at the edge of starvation, but he passed his 'loot' on to the Underground and refused payment or any other form of help. To me and my friends, Mr Artysiewicz has always been the epitome of self-sacrifice and exceptional courage.

I liked my visits to Mr Artysiewicz. I would bring him the *Biuletyn*, pick up and hide on my person the small rectangles of cigarette paper with his carefully scribbled notes; we would talk for a while and I would leave with the satisfying feeling of having accomplished my duty well.

The winter of 1941 was cold. One day, when the temperature dropped to minus fifteen degrees centigrade, I was on my round, walking against the strong wind which drove sharp needles of crystal snow in my face, feeling happy. I was doing something worth while and even though I was cold, the discomfort of struggling with the elements added to my sense of elation; I was, after all, seventeen at the time. It was several days after my encounter with 'the blue', the Polish policeman, and so I had something exciting to tell Mr Artysiewicz. As it happened, he in turn had a gift for me. I don't know whether he had planned it, or whether it was a kind of impromptu response to my latest story. Be it as it may, I left his bedsitter with a 9 mm *Parabellum*, a magnificent weapon, one of the best pistols in the German armoury. I was walking on air. The pistol remained in my possession until the end of the Warsaw Rising in 1944 and even now, half a century later, I am still full of admiration for the man who gave it to me, one who stood head and shoulders above the others.

There were other contacts, other addresses. The intelligence collected on our rounds would go to the chief of our intelligence service, whose name I have now forgotten. Janek Barszczewski, a fellow officer cadet, older than the rest of us at nineteen, had the task of collating the intelligence gathered by our unit. Using large sheets of special, flimsy paper, he would summarise the data on the movements of German troops, their particular units, the numbers of lorries, their identification signs etc.

The Warsaw Citadel was now, of course, occupied by the Germans, but several Polish families still lived in the grounds and among them was one of my old friends. Visiting him gave us a pretext to wander about and make notes on the unit symbols painted on the trucks. This alibi saved our lives when a guard surprised us among the lorries one day. After that, it was left to my friend to collect the required intelligence and to pass it on to us, written as usual on cigarette paper.

All this time random roundups of people and searches of passers-by in the streets were becoming increasingly frequent. One day, just as I left the Citadel and was waiting for my tram on the viaduct over the Gdansk railway station, several German soldiers strolled towards me in a leisurely fashion. But as they approached, their demeanour abruptly changed and, holding a pistol to my head, they searched me thoroughly from top to bottom. This time, luckily, I had placed the all-important flimsies in the small coin compartment of the right hand pocket of my jacket and they missed them. More often I would use the little watch pocket of my trousers as the hiding place, which they did search on this occasion; they found a condom, which made them laugh merrily. They checked my *Arbeitskarte*, the work pass. It was counterfeit, of course, but expertly done. They made a note of the number and let me go. I was greatly relieved.

The latest news from Father was reasonably good, inasmuch as at long last we received a letter from him. It was from a prisoner-of-war camp, written on a special form. We would learn the full story of his experiences much later, after the war, in Paris. The Germans had accused him of treason and put him in front of a court martial, which acquitted him. The trial had been fair and he was even assigned a defending officer. Several days before the appearance, a Gestapo officer came to see him in his cell with a document in his hand. 'Sign here,' he pointed to the dotted line. 'You will be placed under Gestapo protection and thus avoid the courtmartial.' And he added ominously: 'The verdict of the court martial is likely to be death.'

'So be it,' said Father. 'So many Polish officers have already died that one more will not make much difference.'

After his acquittal Father, now classed as a prisoner-of-war, was moved to a camp for officers in some disused fortifications on the old German–Czechoslovak border, whence his first letter came. Later, a few photographs gave us a better idea of the place: it was a special camp for POW officers classed as particularly dangerous.

Subsequently, as a security measure, he would be frequently moved from camp to camp. Father was allowed to write a letter every fortnight and in one of them he gave us the address of a Mrs Ladoś, the wife of a fellow prisoner. We contacted Mrs Ladoś, and met her family. Through them I got to know Janek Płachtowski, later one of my bravest companions. Janek's father had been an army lawyer in Grudziadz, the part of Poland now annexed to the Reich. Expelled from his home town, he and his family moved to the flat belonging to his son-in-law, a relative of the Ladoś family. Soon their home in Żolibórz would become one of our main weapon hideouts.

However, I am anticipating events and must return to my main story. For the time being I divided my time between the school of chemistry, the officers' school and the distribution of clandestine newspapers combined with the collection of intelligence. This kept me busy, but was not very rewarding. One day a cloud of thick black smoke darkened the blue spring sky. A German petrol depot in Gniewkowska Street was on fire. It was a most welcome sight. A sabotage team had blown it up. This was the kind of action I was itching to take part in, but I had no idea how to get in touch with the relevant people.

Everyday life was almost normal. In the morning I would go to school by tram and would do my homework either with Olek or alone. In the tram we often met girls from our school: Renia Wiączek, Elżka Majkowska, Zosia Czechowska. Olek had a weak spot for Renia, while I rather fancied Elżka, a brunette with a good figure.

However, from time to time the ever-threatening reality would reassert itself in the sudden necessity to escape a roundup here, a mass execution there. Additionally, the Germans had begun to herd the Jewish population into the old Jewish quarter of the city. Our tram to the city centre had to pass through that quarter. It would drive through the area at speed, with a German soldier on the running-board, preventing the inhabitants of the ghetto from getting on board or making any contact.

Roundups and searches of tram passengers were a common occurrence. The tram would stop at a road block, where soldiers boarding it would proceed to check documents and thoroughly search each passenger in turn. Anyone trying to escape would be shot on the spot. I witnessed once the death throes of a lad of about my age shot through the abdomen.

One had to be constantly on one's guard. Luckily the telephones were working normally. On one occasion, warned about a roundup at the Żolibórz viaduct, we managed to leave the tram just in time. We made our way to Mrs Koc's flat. Little by little the flat filled with some fifteen young people who had been similarly warned about the roundup and managed to escape. We were aware that the Germans might raid the flat at any moment. 'Let's dance,' suggested Wacek. The electric record player, a novelty before the war, provided welcome entertainment. It also served as a hiding place for Wacek's radio. Soon dancing was in full swing. During this impromptu ball, the telephone suddenly rang. My aunt Alina wanted to speak to me. 'I have been looking for you everywhere,' she said. 'I wanted to remind you to take your raincoat. There is a thunderstorm in the city centre, take great care . . .' This supposedly coded message was meant to deceive any German eavesdroppers.

On this memorable day, some 20,000 people had been deported to Majdanek, a number similar to that other mass deportation of September 1940 to Auschwitz. Now a new camp had been opened, and had to be inaugurated by a mass injection of human misery. By then random arrests in the streets had become part of Warsaw's daily life, complementing, as it were, the targeted arrests of outstanding or professional people such as lawyers, doctors, priests, and individuals suspected of activities against the occupying power.

EIGHT

My Loves, My Friendships and Sabotage

EVEN IN THE MIDST OF THE PRIVATIONS and difficulties of everyday life in the occupied city, we, the seventeen-year-olds, would seek fun and amusement whenever our duties permitted. In the summer, we would find relaxation on the unguarded beach of the Vistula. With my old collapsible rubber canoe taken out of its mothballs and fixed with a sail, the rough waters of the river became our playground for a few hours at a time. It was there that we made friends with a man named Krzysztof, a true sailor, who lived in a hut on the beach and made his living by building and repairing boats.

One day, somebody suggested a swimming race across the river. The Vistula is wide here and its deceptively calm surface conceals strong currents and treacherous eddies. If the other boys wanted to challenge the elements and each other, it was alright with me, but as for myself, in the absence of an accompanying boat and unsure of my prowess, I decided to stay on the beach with Renia.

They left. All was quiet when suddenly, not far from the shore, a little upstream, an object broke the surface of the water. A head? It popped up for a moment, dipped down and then popped up again. One of the boys was drowning! Without a second thought, I dived in and frantically swam to the rescue. Within a minute I was there. 'Grab my shoulders!' I shouted. Before the words were out of my mouth the boy's arms and legs were wrapped, octopus-like, around me and both of us were going down. A self-pitying thought flashed through my mind: 'The other boys must have reached the far side by now and I'll drown here unseen.' With a desperate effort I managed to free myself from the clutches of the drowning man. Luckily, my plight was noticed by a stranger in a canoe and the story had a happy ending: victim number one was pulled, not too much worse for wear, on to the canoe, while I, the prospective victim number two, managed to reach the shore by myself in a state of utter exhaustion.

One day as Renia and I were on our way home from the beach we met one of Renia's schoolmates, an attractive brunette. She greeted us with a delightful smile. The girls chatted, while I stood there dumbstruck, overcome by the girl's beauty. She reminded me vividly of Antonella Lualdi, the Italian actress. Soon, too soon, the girl left us to continue on her way. That was how I met Danka Babińska.

Once again my memory is playing me a trick. I can't quite remember how this 'brief encounter' led to me becoming a frequent visitor in the home of the three attractive women, Mrs Babińska and her two daughters, Zosia and Danka. How did it all come about? God only knows, but it could not have been just by chance. Something new and tremendous had come into my teenage life: a wonderful girl and my first true love. I had, of course, had girlfriends before, but my interest in them waxed and waned like the phases of the moon. This time it hit me like a thunderbolt. I knew it happened to my friends; they were always in love, even though the objects kept changing. Mine didn't – not for a long time.

At the time I was becoming rather disappointed with my role in the Underground; somehow the expected satisfaction was not there. What was rather pretentiously referred to as 'intelligence work' was no doubt useful and dangerous, but it did seem a bit bureaucratic and it did not stretch me enough. I can still see Janek Barszczewski collating and transcribing information from little scraps of cigarette paper onto other, slightly bigger, scraps of cigarette paper. He wanted me to help him, but I wriggled out of this boring task and to his great disgust preferred to go to the beach instead.

The year was 1942. The officers' school and the chemistry classes still took up a lot of my time. Our teachers in the vocational school were excellent, the standard was high, but my position there was precarious. Ignoring German regulations which excluded people with even remote Jewish connections, I had registered under my own name. I have no idea whether any of my schoolmates and teachers knew the truth; as my family was well known in Warsaw, quite a few probably did. However, all through my two years at the school I met no problems and as far as I am aware no one ever thought of denouncing me or even referred to my predicament in private. Similarly, in the suburb where we lived until 1944 many people must have been in the know about our situation. But I will have more to say on the subject later.

One of my schoolmates was Zosia Czechowska, a plump blonde whose generous bust neatly balanced her rather rotund figure. Her exuberance and *joi de vivre* added a touch of colour to the greyness of our daily existence. She had an ardent admirer in Antek Wojciechowski. Antek was in some ways ahead of his time; while the rest of us young males, paid great attention to our appearance, a long jacket, riding breeches and boots being *de rigeur*, he assumed the garb of a tractor driver – a job he had for a while under the Soviet occupation in 1939 – thus pre-empting the fashion of the end, rather than the middle of the twentieth century. Interestingly, our quasi-military attire was considered potentially too provocative and was frowned upon by the Underground authorities.

It was through Antek and Zygmunt that I eventually found my way into *Kedyw*, which was the acronym for *Kierownictwo Dywersji*, or the Directorate of Sabotage. I don't remember exactly how and when Janek told me that he was in contact with the unit responsible for the memorable feat of blowing up the Wehrmacht fuel depot, but I know that I asked him straight away for an introduction to the group. Then nothing happened for a long time, although apparently I had not been rejected. I also learned that Zygmunt knew one of the group leaders, Kazik Jakubowski; though, of course, at the time I did not know his real name. Now, as Zygmunt was the brother of Mundek's widow and a relation of Wacek Koc, I had easy access to him and asked him to intercede for me. Still nothing happened. It was all incredibly difficult – almost as hard as landing a top job nowadays.

The good news came several months later: I was to join a unit of *Kedyw*, planning to blow up a German train on its way to the Russian front. I didn't know at the time that I had been accepted only 'on approval'. The action was to take place on 27 September 1943 in the area of Zalesie Górne, a small settlement near Warsaw. As instructed, I went to the meeting point in a small side street in Żoliborz. A tarpaulin-covered lorry appeared. All fifteen of us slid quickly under the tarpaulin and within minutes we were on our way. My *Parabellum* was inside my belt, and a Sten sub-machine gun hung from my neck in such a way that its rather long magazine passed between my legs. The weapons were thus hidden under a longish coat and one could walk so armed without attracting attention. Unless one met a German patrol, when the only way out was to open the coat fast and use the Sten gun . . . preventively.

Oddly enough, the trickiest and most dangerous phase of the enterprise was the drive. While the number of cars, lorries or vans at the disposal of the Polish population was infinitesimal, road-blocks were many and their locations frequently changed. On the approach of a suspect vehicle, the well hidden German military police had a nasty habit of shooting first and asking questions later. The driver had to be constantly on his guard in order to avoid a trap. The team crowded under the tarpaulin was able to watch the road through the gap between the cover and the driver's cabin, but would be incapable of a quick response in the case of trouble.

However, on this particular occasion the drive was uneventful and at about 10 p.m. we stopped at the edge of a forest. The next part of the journey was on foot and after half an hour's march in single file we reached a clearing. On hearing 'Halt! Who goes there? Password!' in Polish, our leader gave the required response. We filed into the clearing and . . . there, in front of us, was a group of about fifty Polish soldiers in field uniforms, in Polish helmets; no details were visible in the darkness. Rapid orders were rattled out in quick succession. The leader of the forest unit saluted, and together we moved towards the railway embankment.

I have no words to describe the elation of that moment. Even now, almost half a century later, my face tingles, my hair rises and shivers of emotion run up and down my spine. *We are under German occupation, but I am free*! The Polish Army is alive and in a moment we shall take the initiative: we shall destroy the equipment destined for German soldiers on the Russian front. We are no longer a bunch of rabbits hunted on the streets of Warsaw. We can bare our teeth. Never before had I felt so strongly the impact of the word Freedom. That night gave it a special significance. With no intention of invading the realm of pathos, but with a lump in my throat, I can truthfully say that to have lived through that one moment was worth all the risk; in such an instance of supreme exaltation one could meet death face to face without regrets.

Lying close to the sandy soil, we waited some distance from the embankment. Our experts went to fix the device to the rails and returned to wait with us. The device consisted of some plastic explosive and a small dynamo, set to explode at the appropriate moment.

One train passes the spot, then another. Nothing happens. Is there something wrong? Has the device failed?! Have our experts bungled the job? Ludicrous! A third train is coming . . . A powerful detonation! Hurrah! The locomotive rises, shudders, ends up on its side. For a while the deafening whistle of the escaping steam blankets out all other sounds. We rush to the train. I leap on to an open platform and throw a petrol bottle at its load, an army lorry. The vehicle bursts into flames. I throw another bottle. I linger a while. I have no more bottles. They are calling me: 'Stan! Stan! We are backing out!' The train escort opens fire. Bullets whistle by. So what? . . . *I am as happy as one can be.*

I passed the test and was accepted by *Kedyw*. Later, I heard a rumour that originally my inclusion had been delayed because of a silly incident with Antek Wojciechowski. I had met him one day in the street and – as a fellow conspirator, for God's sake – I gave no sign of recognition and I didn't salute him. Apparently he took offence. This story may not be true and, knowing Antek, it does seem rather far fetched.

The officer commanding our Żolibórz *Kedyw* unit was Stasinek Sosabowski. I knew him only by his pseudonym, of course, at the time. Only later did I find out that he was the son of General Sosabowski, Commanding Officer of the Polish parachute brigade in Great Britain. I did know, though, that he was a qualified surgeon, a graduate of the Army Medical School. Having lost an eye in a childhood accident, he couldn't aspire to become a professional soldier and the Army Medical School was the second best. Stasinek and Kazik Jakubowski both spoke in short, characteristically accented sentences. This must have been infectious, as at one stage somebody said to me: 'You must know Kazik. You talk like him.'

At first, I didn't see Stasinek all that often. I had much closer contact with Kazik, Janek and our liaison girls, Zosia and Danka; the latter combined liaison with nursing duties. Danka was a charming wisp of a girl, always smiling and blessed with enormous energy. Rumour had it that she was in love with one of the boys, but that his heart was engaged elsewhere. Also in my unit was my old friend from the Vistula beach, the boat builder and sailor, Krzysztof. He was a few years older than I, very charming and popular with girls. Before the war he had been a student at the Merchant Navy Academy, hence his underground pseudonym of Kolumb or Columbus, to complement his first name of Krzysztof, or Christopher.

In theory we were not supposed to know much about each other – addresses of the other members of the group in particular were taboo. However, within a short time I found my way to the villa occupied by Stasinek and to Kazik's flat, a couple of minutes' walk from mine. I hadn't known any of my new mates before the war, but most of them had been friends, having attended the same school in Żolibórz. To begin with, our contact was limited to our Underground work, but as time went on we got to know each other much better. Intimate friendships were to be forged later, during the

Warsaw Rising, when we spent two months in close proximity; learning to value and rely on each other.

It is not easy now to paint a full picture of those who, like Kazik, died before the Rising. Kazik was tall, handsome and a great patriot. He was a 'doer', uncommonly brave, and he and Stasinek were my heroes at the time. I knew Janek much better, as we had in the past worked together in intelligence. Two or three years my senior, serious and well organised, Janek had a job in the Hartwig Haulage Co., where his characteristically methodical approach to life must have served him well. This trait had also proved priceless in his intelligence collating. But then he took everything seriously, at school, at work or in the Underground. He and his parents and two sisters lived in a villa close to us. Antek was a man full of charm. Columbus was his best friend and between them they could make or repair anything, from weapons to motorcars, from tractors to sailboats. Being so knowledgeable about motors, he and Columbus became our appointed drivers.

At this time I divided my time between *Kedyw*, my decreasing contribution to the intelligence unit and regular (0815 to 1530 hours) work in the Pfeiffer Tannery. Having qualified as a Chemical Technician I had to have practical experience, so I asked Mr Pfeiffer to give me a job in his family business. The Pfeiffer family, tanners for generations, lived in Konstancin and were friends of my grandfather, Stanisław Likiernik, who, as far as I know, had acted in his time for a number of foreign leather merchants and dye producers as their representative in Russia; hence his business connections and friendship with the Pfeiffers was carried on by their respective sons. Disregarding the risk involved in employing me under my own name, Mr Pfeiffer accepted me as a trainee without the slightest hesitation. With the job came a valid certificate of employment; a great additional advantage.

I described earlier the *Kedyw* raid on the train carrying supplies for the German Army on the Russian front, without mentioning the reversal of alliances which had taken place by then. I shall now briefly fill the gap.

All through 1940, when Great Britain was alone in facing the might of Germany, we overestimated her strength. Even the news reports of air raids on London were thought by us to be purely German propaganda. At the same time, the German–Soviet alliance seemed to flourish. The eastern partner was supplying Germany with all kinds of raw materials, rare metals and food. Yet Great Britain stood firm and we were hoping that America would enter the fray soon, though we had no reliable information on the situation in that distant land.

By June 1941 we were aware of the movement of German forces towards the east. It soon became obvious that Hitler was massing armies near the 1939 German–Soviet demarcation line. One day, when passing the loudspeaker on Wilson Square, I heard the announcement: 'Today at dawn, on the order of the Chancellor, Adolf Hitler, the German Army entered the territory of the USSR.' This was great news. We understood at once that this escalation of the war could only be good from our point of view. Naturally we had earlier followed the events in Yugoslavia and Greece with feelings of doom, but the USSR was an opponent of quite a different calibre.

With the USA entering the war later that year, the final victory seemed only a question of time. However, with each day that passed, with the number of victims amongst us constantly growing, our hope of surviving to see the eventual victory was slowly disappearing. I do not aim to provide an exact chronicle of historical events. The relevant details can easily be found elsewhere. I only wish to describe my own feelings and recollections, not always in chronological order, but as they come crowding into my mind, chasing one another.

It was a lovely warm day on 22 June 1941 and I was about to meet my friends on the Vistula beach. With the loudspeaker announcement, a harbinger of good news, still ringing in my ears, I was happily making my way to the rendezvous. But our enjoyment of the beach was short-lived. Afraid of sabotage of the Vistula bridges, the Germans barred all approaches to the river.

At first the news coming from the eastern front was not encouraging. The USSR had not been prepared for defensive war and the resistance offered by the Red Army was melting away like summer snow. Again, we heard the same stories which had appeared at the time of the 1940 Soviet–Finnish war: ill-trained soldiers armed with rifles hanging on bits of string, surrendering to the enemy in their thousands. Soviet POWs started appearing on the streets of Warsaw as columns of a slave labour force. '*Davay zakurit, ryadi Boga*, give us a smoke, for God's sake,' they begged the passers-by. Soon we heard that some prisoners were volunteering for what was to become known as Vlasov's army. We had listened to the miserable renegades in Konstancin nostalgically singing Russian military songs, even those glorifying Stalin. Their betrayal was real enough, but its cause was simple: they had been put in camps surrounded with barbed wire and denied all food and water. The Germans gave them a stark choice: death by starvation, or volunteering for Vlasov's army. Some chose differently: rumours reached us that thousands of Soviet captives in the camps threw themselves against the barbed wire and that, in spite of great losses to machine-gun fire, many managed to escape and join partisan units.

Thirsting as we were for news, our sources of information were few. All the wireless receiver/transmitters were in the hands of the Underground, used to maintain contact with the West. Radios in private hands were a rarity, their possession punishable by death. Hence the immense popularity of the clandestine press, any scrap of news being passed from hand to hand, from mouth to mouth. So even misinformation, often undeservedly optimistic, helped us to cope with the wretched reality.

Social contact between the Polish population and the occupying forces was non-existent. In trams, half the carriages were invariably reserved *Nur für Deutsche*. The Germans had their own shops, well provided with everything we could obtain only on the black market. They largely avoided Polish restaurants and coffee houses. We lived in two separate worlds: it was them and us. Our only points of contact – the roundups, the searches, the executions – were those of the hunter and his game. *Kedyw* did on a few occasions reverse this set-up and, though regrettably only for brief periods, we were able to defend ourselves, or, even better, to attack.

Street patrols were increasingly frequent. Sometimes the SS men would pass by without giving you a glance. On other occasions they would demand your *Kennkarte*, the compulsory ID, with a sub-machine gun pointed at your belly. One had to comply and to keep calm. One day, in Żolibórz, almost on our doorstep, I was thus stopped: '*Papieren*,' one of them barked. I gave the SS man my *Kennkarte*. It was a counterfeit, made only the day before and, through our shortage of ink, the rubber stamp was the wrong colour. Calmly, I looked the SS man straight in the eye. Would he notice? My luck held. He didn't. Had he done so, my biography would have been very much shorter.

In true roundups passers-by would be herded together, told to face the wall, arms up, palms on the wall, and thoroughly searched for weapons, for clandestine press and other forbidden items; the aim of a roundup would generally be the provision of hostages, concentration camp fodder, or slave labour for the Reich.

It would be an impossible task to describe in detail the

vicissitudes and disasters of the years of occupation. The risk and the danger were constant, even for those genuinely uninvolved in any clandestine activity. Most arrests were arbitrary, some were based on unwarranted suspicions. Following interrogation, the more savage the less there was to confess, the surviving prisoner would find himself in a concentration camp. Moving about the streets of Warsaw was therefore a risky pastime. One had to be constantly vigilant, even more so if one happened to be carrying any contraband.

NINE

The Warsaw Ghetto.
My Work in the Pfeiffer Tannery

THE GERMAN ANTI-SEMITIC POLICY UNFOLDED SLOWLY, with all its inevitable thoroughness. At first the Jews were confined to a strictly circumscribed area. Later that area was surrounded by a wall, though for a while its gates remained open. The northern tramline connecting Żolibórz with the city centre crossed the Jewish quarter, and trams would pass through it at great speed without stopping.

Eventually the ghetto, by then reduced in size, was sealed off from the rest of the city. Its gates were closed and the tram ran along a high brick wall concealing the view of the forbidden area. At times, especially in the beginning, groups of Jewish workers, identified by arm-bands depicting the star of David, would be marched under guard in and out of the ghetto to work. Later all communication between the ghetto and the rest of the city would be cut. Some clandestine contact remained, but it was difficult and sporadic.

The ghetto lived a life apart, with a Jewish police, Jewish authorities and the Jewish Council (*Judenrat*). Factories working for the German Army employed skilled Jewish workers. Soon, the barrier between the Jewish ghetto and the remainder of the city, colloquially known in the ghetto as the Aryan side, became well-nigh impenetrable. But even at that stage nobody could have imagined the blows still to come and the eventual fate of this enclave, inhabited originally by some 300,000 people; the number was to be greatly increased later by the influx of Jews expelled from the environs of the capital.

The Germans used a sophisticated, scientifically designed method of oppression. Each successive turn of the screw was carefully gauged to leave a glimmer of hope. First, the Jews in the ghetto were given a semblance of self-government. Then the deportations started building up. At first they concerned only the sick and the destitute. The Jewish police, who had to provide the quotas for deportations, were working under the illusion that they and their families would be given a protected status in return for collaboration. The deportees, too, were deceived into thinking that they were being taken to work somewhere in the east. These unfortunate people, exhausted by starvation and disease, treated with unprecedented brutality by the armed Nazi troops, allowed themselves to be rounded up and crowded into cattle wagons with little resistance.

In Jeziorna, near Konstancin, the town of my childhood, the Germans expelled the entire Jewish population in a single day. In the process Mr Dębski, my venerable tailor of patriarchal appearance, had his silver beard torn out by a soldier. Andrzej Mularczyk, now a writer, described how at the age of ten he saw an escaping Jewish child chased and kicked to death by the Germans in front of his house. The sight has haunted him ever since. Many Polish Jews tried to find refuge outside the ghetto. With forged IDs, necessary to hide their often typically Jewish names, thousands would find shelter with friends, or sometimes with strangers unaware of their origin. However, among the mostly blond and blue-eyed Slav people a pronounced Semitic appearance was difficult to disguise. Even a short walk in the street could end in death. Many lived in confinement for years, often in tiny but ingeniously constructed hiding places. House searches were a constant threat. Once discovered, the Jews, as well as the entire family sheltering them, would be taken to their deaths.

In the second half of the war there were two separate armed risings in Warsaw. Dr Edelman, the deputy leader of the Jewish Ghetto Rising of April 1943, calculated that even after the Polish Home Army Warsaw Rising of August–September 1944, there were some 12,000 Jews left in Warsaw; these could have survived only by the good deeds of at least 100,000 Poles. Not a bad record for a city of, at the time, some 700,000 Polish inhabitants.

The Żolibórz villa belonging to Mrs Koc, the mother of my friend Wacek, was a hive of clandestine activity. All her three children, two sons and a daughter, were involved in the Underground resistance. One day in September 1939 her younger son, Andrzej, thirteen at the time, returned home with a rifle which afterwards remained hidden in the cellar. Later he constructed a radio receiver and concealed it inside the record player. A small room on the first floor was occupied by a man who later proved to be none other than General Spychalski, one of the leaders of the communist Underground. In the basement lived a Mr Balcerzak with his two sons. They were my workmates in the Pfeiffer tannery, and I had introduced them to Mrs Koc. There, in the basement of her villa, they ran a small illegal tannery to supplement their meagre earnings. In addition, at least ten assorted 'non-Aryans' either lived in the villa or used it as their official address. 'Mrs Koc's private ghetto,' we quipped. But Wacek's mother was one of the elite who refused to accept defeat and who continued to be active in the resistance movement. Mrs Koc, a teacher of Polish literature and a woman of great charm and intelligence, became a member of the Underground without even realising it. A rifle to be hidden; an illegal radio receiver; a Jewish friend needing help . . . She did all this, as it was her way of remaining true to herself. Even if the likely price was death. She was gentle and vulnerable. She worried greatly about her children, but was reconciled to their dangerous clandestine activity. I cannot but remember her with the greatest affection. Her home was for many of us a warm welcoming haven; the warmer and the more charming for the presence of Jaga, Wacek's older sister.

In the summer of 1942, I started my one-year paid traineeship in the Pfeiffer tannery. My co-trainee was Stefan Graf, one of my vocational school classmates. Our job was to familiarise ourselves as workers with all the stages of leather production. It was difficult in the beginning, but we gained much useful experience. This was my first close contact with industry, with workers, with the life of a factory and my first real exposure to manual work. I encountered no great problems, except that my love of books was rather difficult to explain to my workmates. 'What's a book good for?' they would tease me: 'To keep a glass on.' A glass full of vodka, of course.

Tanning was quite a lengthy process. The bovine skins, once depilated, were immersed in a special tank. My first job was to remove them after soaking. Each skin would first be raised on a long pole to the surface of the tank. Two of us would then grab it by the head and the tail ends respectively. The two places to be got hold of had to be instantly identified, which was not as easy at it sounds. Once the skin was lifted out, we would fold it lengthwise in two and throw it on a heap. In the next stage the skins, folded in four, had to be taken on flat wheelbarrows to another building for processing. But wet skins were slippery and to balance them on the conveyance required skill. The norm was five skins per trip. Experts managed ten. For me, three was a lot. Having moved their three wheelbarrow loads of ten skins each, my workmates waited for me, still struggling

with six loads of five. My clumsy attempts to cope would be met
with outbursts of laughter, at least in the early days. Even after all
the depilation and soaking, the skins still seemed to be alive and
would wilfully slide off my wheelbarrow. I had to refold them and
reload – and the next moment they would be on the floor again.
Painstakingly reloaded, they would slide off once more. More
laughter. But in a few days I caught up and managed to keep the
slippery load under control.

Winter came early that year. The October–November
temperatures dropped to below freezing. We worked in the open
and our hands and entire right arms were permanently wet from
fishing the skins out of the tank. In temperatures of minus ten to
minus fifteen degrees centigrade and occasionally even minus
twenty degrees centigrade this was no joke. Luckily I discovered a
barrel with hot water, replenished constantly by condensing steam.
Every so often I would run to it and dip my frozen fingers in the
almost boiling water. To my great surprise, the frostbite on my
hands, contracted the previous winter, miraculously healed; contrast
baths, an old wives' remedy for frostbite, really did work.

My next job was in the drying hall. It was the same hall in which
my father had fought his first duel all those years ago. When they
reached the drying hall the skins, just removed from the tannin bath,
would be cut lengthwise in half. Next, the half-skins were nailed to
a beam about three metres long, and then the heavy beam with its
suspended skins, had to be lifted on to special supports, fixed on
successive levels. The drying process started at the ground level.
Then, at intervals, the beams, one by one, had to be lifted on to the
next level . . . and then on to the next one . . . and on to the one
higher again. This was done by two men, precariously balanced on
planks fixed across the hall, each holding one end of the beam.
Moving the beams from level one to level two was not difficult, you
just had to lift them over your head. But the highest level was some
eight to ten metres above the ground and I was terrified – the void
under my feet was fearsome, worse to me than anything else,
perhaps even worse than the war. It was warm in the drying hall, but
after a few days I asked to be transferred back outside. I preferred
solid ground under my feet, even in more than ten degrees of frost.

I could fill a whole volume describing the work in the tannery.
On changing from one shop to another one had to sweeten one's
prospective workmates and instructors with *bimber*, or moonshine,
a foul home brew. First one cut any old bottle with a red-hot wire
tightened half-way round it and rapidly cooled with water. The

bottom half made a passable glass; used with skill it would not even cut your lips. Everybody in turn would fill it with *bimber* and drink to the health of the others. Another toast would be raised to our future. One could not quarrel with tradition.

To the chagrin of my latter-day French compatriots, I could never tell the difference between that brew and their best brandy.

On some of my tannery jobs I produced more than the usual quota of rejects. For instance, to remove the excess thickness of a piece of leather one had to use a special curved knife. But in my hands the knife would not keep still, it would go right through the piece in so many places that the end result would be more like a colander than a usable piece of leather. But so what? The leather was intended for the German Army after all.

We spent the last six months in the finishing hall. Here, high heaps of half-finished leather provided ideal hiding places where occasionally Stefan Graf and I could revise our French vocabulary undisturbed. At the time we applied ourselves seriously to learning French and English. One never knew, perhaps one day foreign languages would come in useful . . .

In parallel with the work in the tannery, I attended the clandestine university. With Olek, Renia, Danka and several others we enrolled at the faculty of chemistry. Again, as in the *gimnazjum*, lectures were held in the afternoon in private flats and houses. As the tannery work finished at 3.30 p.m., I just about managed to make it if I hurried. Soon, though, I discovered that higher maths and physics were not my cup of tea. And in addition, the whiff of the tannery, which inevitably followed me wherever I went, didn't find favour with our teachers.

On one occasion, I rushed into the lecture room after my first day in a new shop. Inevitably, a bottle of home brew had had to be split with my new workmates. The normal whiff of the tannery combined with that of cheap moonshine proved too much for the class, while the maths proved too much for me. With Dutch courage, halfway through the Maclaurin's series, I loudly voiced my misgivings: 'What's the point of all this? I don't understand a thing. Neither do the others, I bet . . . Anyway, who cares?' From then on, the clandestine university and I had to go our separate ways.

I was happy with my decision. Using the knowledge gained at the university, I made a simple calculation of *a priori* probabilities. This showed that my chances of survival were close to zero. So why should I let maths kill me bit by bit? The Germans were bound to do the job much more efficiently. However, just in case, I decided to continue my study of foreign languages. Olek and some other of my friends had been doing so for some time; keen as they were, they also passed the first and second year university exams in chemistry. But alas, as far as they were concerned, my probability calculation had proved correct – almost all of them perished. I, perversely, survived. And the French and the English did come in useful.

At about that time a short strike took place in the tannery. One more German order was proclaimed, requiring every family to give up all old metal in their possession. I didn't even learn the reason for the strike until after the tools had been downed: the workforce expected the tannery to provide them with old metal to render unto Caesar. A hundred workers gathered, blocking the entrance to the manager's office. But after Mr Pfeiffer appeared and spoke sense to the assembled workers, the strike collapsed. I had resented the solidarity that was expected of all, even in a case where the demand was quite absurd. The episode also opened my eyes to the inferiority complex of the industrial worker. To my mind one should not have started a strike without a good reason, but once it was done, one ought to have stuck to one's guns, while this rather frivolous strike ended after only a few sensible words from the boss.

After one year I'd had enough of the tannery. Work in and on behalf of the Underground took up more and more of my time, and I would have liked to dedicate myself to it totally. Yet I still had to go to work and earn a living.

Our factory was situated in Okopowa Street, at the edge of the ghetto; it was practically an enclave within it. The windows of the office building looked out onto it. One day our foreman, a grey-haired older man and by no means a Jew-lover, came into our workshop in a state of shock, white as a sheet and unsteady on his legs. A noise had reached him from outside the window. He looked out. German soldiers had rounded up a group of Jewish men, women and children, and made them kneel and form a queue. As the poor wretches moved forward on their knees, an SS man with a pistol in his hand shot them one by one. Other Jews were made to move the bodies out of the way of the slowly advancing queue. The terrible sight made our manager shudder with rage and loathing.

In the spring of 1943 I finally left the tannery and, at long last, I was a free agent. I had had enough of factory work and of the university. Luckily, Mr Pfeiffer proved generous enough to let me keep my document stating that I was employed in an enterprise working for the Germans. It was an ID with a photograph and an expiry date. In the near future, this document was to prove very important.

TEN

The Underground as a Way of Life

I AM NOT SURE EXACTLY HOW AND WHEN IT HAPPENED, but eventually I became a full-time member of the Underground. I received small amounts of money, enough to live on. What was I doing day by day? I would be hard pushed to give an account of my activities, except in a very general way. I spent a lot of time cycling round Warsaw, meeting people, passing on and receiving intelligence in friendly shops, secret haunts and safe-houses, alerting participants for specific jobs, or generally doing the donkey-work involved in planning and preparing various actions. My first autonomous task was to organise the construction of a wooden garage to conceal our lorry. Procuring the necessary timber, transporting it to the small designated plot in Czerniaków, on the riverside, and organising the workforce without arousing suspicion, was far from easy. I was very proud of myself when the task was successfully completed.

I had a lot of free time on my hands, but I had to be on duty near a phone, either at home or in a friendly flat, waiting for a call, rather like a fireman. Messages were in code. The number of so-called 'jobs' kept increasing. Today I could not possibly list them all. They were not all of the same importance or interest.

Waiting by the phone was tedious. The only possible pastime was reading. I decided to restrict my reading to French books, and to read them from cover to cover. Zola's *Nana*, which I found in my father's library, was easy. *Au Bonheur des Dames* by the same author, in an elegant binding with my aunt's cipher A.L., proved a much harder nut to crack. I spent a month on this book, with the dictionary forever in my hands. But I did not give up. During that month the telephone provided double deliverance: at last a job was coming my way, and I could also put down the *Bonheur des Dames*, at least for a while. However, the intellectual effort involved proved worth my while: without me realising it, French words, expressions and phrases somehow entered my head, and stayed there.

In between actions we had to deal with such problems as organising arms caches, hiring lodgings under different names, procuring counterfeit documents and perhaps even some 'true false' documents. All of this was difficult, but necessary for continuing the fight and essential for survival. As part of those activities I managed to acquire a new 'true false' identity. It was really quite simple. Through a lay official of a church in Bielany, I obtained the birth certificate of a stillborn baby with the name Henryk Wichowski. Thus armed I went to the German ID Bureau, filled in the application form for a *Kennkarte*, added the required mug shots and hey presto, I walked out with a perfectly legal document issued by a German authority.

At the time, then, I was in possession of a document in my own name, bearing my true address, several other *Kennkarten* also in my name but showing the addresses of different legitimate lodgings (one was not permitted to spend the night in a lodging other than one's own; it was important for the name and address to tally in case of a house search), and now also a perfectly genuine *Kennkarte* in the name of Henryk Wichowski. When going into action one never carried any document – in death, one had to remain anonymous. Showing one's papers, while carrying a pistol inside one's belt, was out of the question.

After the train action in Zalesie Górne one of our first jobs, and rather a distressing one, was to kidnap a Pole condemned by the Underground Court to death for denouncing Polish officers to the Germans and to carry out the verdict. At the beginning of the occupation all Polish officers had been ordered to register, and the ones who did were promptly sent to prisoner-of-war camps. The majority did not and had to stay in hiding. The traitor, whose name I do not recall, lived in our quarter. We decided to seize him in a quick operation, get him into our car and take him out of town for execution. This was my first job of that kind. We stopped the traitor's car in Mickiewicz Street. He refused to come with us. Kazik Jakubowski fired his gun and we had to make ourselves scarce. We pushed the man, now more compliant, into our car and drove to a forest north of Warsaw. In the condemned man's wallet we found a list of officers' names and addresses, obviously those he planned to denounce.

Luckily I was not included in the execution squad, but served as a lookout. As was appropriate for the occasion, I wore a German police uniform, complete with a helmet, and had the regulation sub-machine gun in my hands. Camouflaged near a forest path, I was all ears. Suddenly, steps . . . voices . . . Several peasant women came out of the thicket, laden with bundles, packs on their backs. Chicken, geese, butter, eggs . . . on their way to the black market. Though illegal, this was the main supply line for Warsaw through all the years of the occupation. The official ration cards might just as well have been kept as souvenirs, for all they were worth. In the four years of the occupation the Germans provided the city with no more than four months' worth of food. To survive, the inhabitants of Warsaw had to use the black market.

True to my role of a German policeman, I shouted 'Halt!' Terrified, the women begged me to let them go, in Polish of course. 'Raus, schnell, verfluchte!' My limited German vocabulary just about fitted the occasion. My prospective victims needed no encouragement; they ran away, no doubt amazed by the benevolence of the gendarme who didn't even demand a single goose as the price of their freedom. Smuggling of unlicensed food, breeding non-registered pigs, could cost the farmer his life. In my place, a real gendarme would, at his most benevolent, confiscate the goods, and at worst let go with his sub-machine gun. Searches of trains often ended in the shooting of women and men travelling with contraband food supplies.

Patrols of ten to fifteen soldiers would check documents and carry out searches in the streets. One day, Janusz Płachtowski and I were walking down a minor street in our quarter. At a turning we noticed a German patrol entering the street from a side road about 200 metres away. We stopped and unhurriedly turned round. Somebody signalled to us from a window: 'They saw you. They are going to shoot.' We turned round again and proceeded calmly on our way. It so happened that we had a large sum of Home Army money in Polish złotys on us; a good enough reason to arrest us. Yet we had no choice but to go on. 'Hände hoch!' a brisk search. They opened Janusz's attaché case first, and found . . . a pile of anti-Semitic leaflets – a horrible Jewish profile and an enormous louse, with a legend underneath saying: 'Louse = Jew = Typhus.' An outburst of laughter. They approved of our reading matter. We were safe.

There was a simple reason for the anti-Semitic literature in Janusz's attaché case. In order to be legitimately able to move in the streets of Warsaw after curfew, Janusz had become a fireman. A stack of the leaflets was found in his fire station. The paper used for them was just the right quality for personal hygiene, and toilet paper was in short supply. Which goes to show that in some circumstances, the shortage of a basic item like that may actually save one's life.

One of my daily tasks was the moving of ammunition and explosives. It was a dangerous, yet tedious job. One day our lorry brought a box of detonators to a designated drop-off place. From there I had to take it to Stasinek's villa, 200 to 300 metres away. Some donkey-work. The load was heavy and kept slipping down my back. It was quite awkward to keep in place while I attempted to walk nonchalantly in order not to attract the attention of passers-by and neighbours. I still wonder whether the box would have exploded on hitting the pavement. Luckily, I reached my friend's door without finding out.

All that time I was very much in love with Danka Babińska, the girl who first caught my eye during our brief encounter on the riverside. We used to attend the same lectures at the clandestine university. She had another admirer who would wait for her after classes. He had the advantage of being an old beau, but I counted on the attraction of novelty. Never losing hope, I started chatting her up. She had a wonderful figure and I couldn't keep my eyes off her. When she smiled, which she often did, her regular teeth gleamed white and small wrinkles appeared at the corners of her almond-shaped eyes. Her father was a colonel in the cartographic service of the Polish Army; he had managed to escape to the West and was stationed in Scotland. She lived with her mother, still a very attractive woman, and her sister, Zosia. Danka had a dark, Mediterranean kind of beauty, while blonde Zosia was a typical Slav girl. Soon Danka and I were doing our homework together, either at her place or mine, and I was becoming a part-time member of the Babiński household; but the curfew being set for 8 p.m., I had to dash home early.

My tactical position improved further when I learned that there was a room to let on the ground floor of their villa. The flat belonged to a retired general. I knocked on the door sporting a blue cap with gold piping round the crown, the kind of headgear worn by employees of gas, electricity and water services. I also had a proper employment certificate; somebody else was collecting the salary, in exchange for the fully verifiable document of a municipal worker. And so Henryk Wichowski became a legitimate lodger in the general's flat. I was able to sleep there during the day and disappear for the night. My work status provided full explanation.

The general, lately of the Austro-Hungarian Army, was a fierce loyalist, opposed to armed resistance and very pleased to have such an exemplary tenant. My new abode had a window looking on to the garden, allowing weapons and explosives to be taken in or out of my room without attracting attention; I was thus invariably 'clean' while using the front door. Last but not least, I could spend entire evenings upstairs, despite the curfew and to the despair of my rival.

Mrs Babińska tolerated my frequent presence, and the two girls were charming; briefly, but for the war, life could have been very pleasant. Yet I was not getting anywhere with Danka. It was all devilishly difficult. There was a Jewish couple from Lwów hiding at the Babińskis at that time. The wife was encouraging: 'She loves you,' she would assure me. 'She definitely prefers you to the other one.' But I was waiting for Danka to confirm it herself. It did seem a long wait.

At the time, I had three lodgings. One, at 27 Mickiewicz Street, was in my own name. The other, in Danka's house at 40 Śmiała Street, was in the name of Henryk Wichowski. The third one, in Grzybowska Street in the city centre, was a sub-let in the flat of a young couple with a small child, who lived in strained circumstances and in constant fear of the Germans. At first they were pleased to have a quiet and frequently absent tenant – until one day they discovered that Henryk Wichowski was actually the young Mr Likiernik from Konstancin. I had been recognised by a Konstancin girl employed in a neighbourhood laundry. My landlady guessed that I was working for the Underground. This made her anxious, but she didn't show me the door. I have recently heard that these brave people and their child survived the 1944 Warsaw Rising in which over 160,000 civilians and 35,000 soldiers of the Underground perished.

The job of preparing successive actions was time-consuming. Maintaining the necessary contacts, assembling the team at short notice and preferably without using the phone, was a complex task. I made much use of my bicycle, which proved the best and quickest way of moving about. As letter boxes we used the small patisseries run by the wives of officers presently serving abroad and thus able to send home food parcels from Great Britain, via neutral Portugal. The wives teamed up to produce mouth-watering cakes. This was the life! For weeks at a time I lived on mocha tarts, chocolate gateaux and cheese cakes.

Letters from Father, written on special forms, would reach us about once a month or once a fortnight. As I mentioned before, Father had put us in touch with Mrs Ladoś and her relations, the Płachtowskis, who, expelled from Pomerania, found refuge in Warsaw. Their son, Janusz, two years my junior, was accepted on my recommendation by the Warsaw division of *Kedyw*. On his first action – that of blowing up a train – Janusz did not leave my side. After the explosion, the enemy *matériel* destroyed and our task accomplished, we ran back to our lorry, fired at by the Germans from behind the overturned wagons. Bullets whistled round us. Suddenly, I felt Janusz's arm round my neck. He kissed my cheek. He was in high heaven – at last he had taken part in a real action. I understood only too well.

All in all I took part in four train actions, two of which I remember very well. Even though both operations followed the usual pattern, the selection of participants for one of them had been rather unorthodox. The action was to be carried out by another unit of the AK (The Home Army) supplemented by four co-opted members of *Kedyw*, including me. Several hours before the appointed time, I went to Kazik Jakubowski's house to fetch the required grenades. He met me on the doorstep: 'You are not going. I am going in your place. The Germans have arrested my friend, Czechowski (Zosia's brother). I have to avenge him.' I refused to yield, even though Kazik was my superior, but eventually he suggested tossing a coin. He won. Still I would not agree. 'It's my turn and I am going,' I obstinately insisted. Even if the job had seemed suicidal, I would not have given way. Stasinek lived round the corner and so I ran to his place. He went to see Kazik, they discussed it at length, and eventually it was I who went.

The driver, whose pseudonym was Rymwid, though unfortunately not our Antek, assured us that he knew all about cars. We were soon proceeding in a saloon car stolen from the Germans. For some reason, a small red light on the dashboard would not go off. 'It's okay,' insisted our driver. I had my doubts, but he knew better . . . We had to cross the Poniatowski Bridge, which was under constant surveillance. Doing so would have been dangerous even with Antek at the wheel. Everything was under control, however, until the Saska Kępa crossroad, where the engine stalled. It refused to restart. We had to get out and push. It was a wide street with not another car in sight. Virtually all motorised traffic was German; and here were we, two young civilian men pushing a car. Very suspicious. Moreover, my *Parabellum*, with its strap round my neck and wedged in my belt, had detached itself and was dangling between my legs.

Luckily, not a soul was in sight and we were not challenged. The engine started and once more we were moving, but the red light was still on. We joined the other unit in the woods and the rest of the operation went as planned. Fogel, an excellent motor mechanic from the other team, checked our car. A short circuit had exhausted the battery. To start us on the sandy forest tract, the other team had to push us again and again before our engine finally fired. Any delay could prove catastrophic. But happily it was Fogel who took over the driving, and without meeting a single patrol we arrived back in Warsaw at dawn all in one piece.

About that time, coming home one evening well before the curfew, I found two men waiting for me, one in the navy-blue uniform of the Polish police, the other in civvies, also a Pole.

'Documents,' he extended his hand. 'And drop your trousers.'

The latter examination proved conclusive – I was not circumcised. 'Where is your father?' asked the policeman.

'In a German *Oflag*.'

'Oh, well,' he looked askance at the plainclothes man. Then he turned to me again. 'Have you any tenants?'

'Yes.'

'Be on your guard. We received information that there were Jews living at this address, but as it does not apply to you,' he referred to the result of his examination, 'we will be on our way.'

I didn't know, and wouldn't want to know, my tenant's real name but as soon as the two men left, I told him about the visit. He moved out straight away. I also decided to keep away from this particular lodging for a few days. The episode prompted me to work out an escape plan. I took to arranging my clothes in such a way that I could dress almost instantly. I planned to run to my balcony, leap over its concrete partition to the next balcony, then through the next door flat to another staircase. A woman of about twenty-five, whose husband was a prisoner-of-war, lived in that flat. One day, I decided to test my escape route – without warning my neighbour. Perhaps deep down I hoped for an adventure of quite another kind. But in vain. She was there. She agreed to my escape plan. The result was unequivocal: escape – yes, hanky-panky – no.

Some time later we were warned that the Gestapo had been asking about us during a house search in the neighbourhood. The risk of staying put had become too great and we decided to leave the flat. I had to remain in Warsaw, but I did have other lodgings, or I could spend nights at the Płachtowskis. But Mother had to move out. Roman Mularczyk's uncle, a Warsaw lawyer and our family friend, had returned to his birthplace, Boryczówka, a village in south-eastern Poland near Tarnopol. It seemed just the right kind of place for Mother. Travel was difficult but still possible. So I found myself in Warsaw on my own.

In Boryczówka, Mother tended the cows and helped Mrs Mularczyk to look after the children; she managed to adapt fairly well to country life.

Our flat stood empty, except for one room sub-let to a lady. The weapons were in their hiding place. Our housekeeper came occasionally to tidy up. As all was quiet and no one had looked for us, after several months we decided to move back. Relying on my old escape route, I moved in first. Mother returned to Warsaw some six months later. She wanted to be with me. Besides, she had had enough of country life – in that part of occupied Poland, Ukrainian nationalists presented an increasing threat to the Polish inhabitants.

About that time we got news of the arrest and death under torture of one of our former tenants. As I never knew his name and don't remember his pseudonym, let's call him Piotr. A friend of Mundek, my first superior in the Underground, Piotr was a chemistry graduate and before the war had worked in a sugar refinery. Taken prisoner-of-war, he managed to escape. As he spoke fluent German, the Underground entrusted him with the task of organising the escape of officers from camps in Germany. He travelled on either German or Ukrainian documents. One day he returned from Berlin with a small facial wound: the result of allied bombing of the German capital. This was wonderful news. And straight from the horse's mouth. At last, Germany was getting a dose of its own medicine.

Piotr's original escape from the camp is an interesting story in itself. One way or another, he had managed to procure a German uniform. A fellow prisoner, a sculptor, made him an exact replica in wood of a German rifle. Thus uniformed and armed, he insinuated himself into an escort of four Polish officers being taken to a court of law. The stratagem could only work thanks to Piotr's fluent German. Helped by some German soldiers travelling to the eastern front, all five escapees returned safely to Poland. Piotr's fiancée was selling cakes in a patisserie across the street from our house. She was naturally overjoyed by his return. Regrettably soon after, I was passing by and saw her in tears. At first I didn't understand . . . but one never asked direct questions in the circumstances.

This episode reminds me of another one, much more trivial, but which could have easily been the end of me. An Underground

Minor Sabotage Unit had covered Warsaw houses with graffiti, just one word; OCTOBER. The anniversary of the creation of the General Government by the Germans was coming in October, and the mysterious word was meant to indicate that something was brewing and therefore undermine German morale. Tension was rising. On the anniversary day the streets of Warsaw were crawling with German patrols. An open lorry was moving slowly down our street, with two rows of gendarmes watching both sides, rifles at the ready.

I happened to be standing in the window. The lorry stopped in front of our house, the soldiers leapt down and rushed up our staircase. Seeing this, I ran up the stairs to the door leading to the flat roof. I knew that the door was kept locked, so I opened the window to the right of it. I jumped – it was the fourth floor – on to the wide balustrade on the left, forgetting the void beneath me. I kept watching the three German helmets below. Luckily, the soldiers had not noticed my acrobatics. The rest of the patrol were searching all the flats, including ours, looking for a young man who had apparently stood in front of our house and, as the patrol went by, whistled at them, or made a threatening sign. Having reached the flat roof, bent in half, I sprinted to the nearest trap-door and let myself into the attic. The space was about one metre high. Half an hour later, after the gendarmes had gone, I returned home by the same route.

Later that day, I went across the street to buy some cakes. 'I saw you on the roof earlier,' said the young woman. 'Just as well the gendarme posted on the pavement here did not look up . . .'

I would have made a very easy target.

ELEVEN

A German Visit. A Botched Job

OF THE YEARS 1943 AND 1944 till the outbreak of the Warsaw Rising on 1 August 1944, I can recall only isolated incidents, such as the *Kedyw* operations and events directly concerning my mother and myself. My memory of this period is not unlike a distant view of mountains: a few peaks rising here and there in a sea of clouds.

Mother and I were under constant threat of house searches and arrest. This very nearly happened in early February 1944. On the morning of the fourth, there were no meetings to attend and I was at home on my own. Suddenly I remembered that my employment certificate was due to expire at the end of the month. With nothing better to do, I made my way to the Pfeiffer tannery hoping to have my papers stamped with a new date. One of the staff, whom I knew well, took one look at the document and showed me the date: 'Your certificate is valid till the end of March, you need not have come yet.'

'Quite right, my mistake. I'll be back in a month's time.'

With time on my hands I went round the tannery to see my old friends the Balcerzaks, father and son, and Stefan Graf, who was still working there. We spent about an hour chatting. I was about to leave when Stefan was called to the porter's lodge to take a telephone call. He came running back. 'Don't go home,' he called. 'You've had a visit from the Gestapo.'

It was Mrs Hetlinger, our neighbour, who had phoned with the warning. Anxious about Mother, I immediately called Mrs Hetlinger back. Mother was still out. She had left in the morning to do her voluntary work helping to pack parcels for prisoners in Auschwitz. When the Germans came, our home help had opened the door and told them that Mother and I were at work and wouldn't be back until evening. Surprisingly, instead of setting the usual trap by waiting for our return and preventing the housekeeper warning us, the Germans believed the old woman and left. She ran upstairs to Mrs Hetlinger, who passed the warning on to me, having guessed that I could be found in the tannery, and then helped to get our clothes and other small items of personal use out of our flat.

The Gestapo returned in the evening. The flat was empty. Furious, they sealed the entrance and, on leaving, told the caretaker: 'Should we find the seal broken, you'll go straight to Auschwitz.' Thus warned, the caretaker assiduously watched our door and the staircase.

We had had a lucky escape. Mother remained at liberty and so did I – as a result of my mistimed visit to the tannery. She went to stay with her old friend, Mrs Strasburger. By this time the lady had married her commanding officer in the Underground, and her name was now Olewińska. The couple lived in our old house in Konstancin, the site of Father's arrest in 1939. I now had to create a new identity for Mother. This was not much of a problem as my cousin, Staś Wojecki, had become an expert in such matters. And so, with Mother's new counterfeit *Kennkarte* in the name of Wanda Malinowska, which was only short of a photo to appear genuine, I took a tram to Narutowicz Square. Surprisingly, except for the driver and myself, the tram was empty. Did this mean there was a roundup on the line? People must have known about it, but having been the only one waiting at the tram stop, I had not been warned.

The next minute the German road block came into view. The policemen were making signs for the driver to stop. Mother's incomplete *Kennkarte* in my pocket would have meant interrogation, beating, concentration camp, or worse. I threw it under another seat. Wrapped in white paper, it remained very conspicuous. Suddenly the tram accelerated – by the driver's whim, or because of me? I shall never know. The policemen had to jump aside and the tram passed at speed. I recovered the *Kennkarte*, warmly shook the driver's hand and gave him all the money I had on me. Words were unnecessary. We understood each other. Another lucky escape.

I still had a problem; I needed to get back to the sealed flat to retrieve a few things. Some items of a strictly non-kosher nature, like my *Parabellum*, a Sten sub-machine gun and a sum of USA dollars belonging to AK, the Home Army, were left concealed in a hiding place built for the purpose by an expert cabinet maker, an elderly gentleman working for the Underground. He had made it by lifting several blocks of the parquet floor in one of our rooms and clearing a space underneath by removing the rubble insulating our floor from the ceiling below. He then glued the loose blocks together to make a hinged flap, which could be sprung open by inserting a thin nail file in a particular place. I understand that this secret hiding place is still being used, though in a more prosaic manner, by the present occupier of our old flat.

The flat was on the third, or top floor, of a big apartment block, with a frontage of about 500 metres. I had already escaped from the flat once, and didn't see why I shouldn't get in using the same route. From the roof one ought to be able to get onto our balcony and then into the flat. One night a friend and I did just that, without too much difficulty. We emptied the hiding place. We also took some mementoes, such as photos, the only photos I now have from before the war, several books, and a portrait of my father painted by an Englishman in Colditz, the notorious castle housing the high-escape-risk Allied prisoners of war.

The flat's main entrance door opened inward, onto our corridor. Before leaving, just for fun, we blocked it. We left the corridor chock-a-block with tables, chairs and sofas. The seals on the door remained intact and the caretaker could not be held responsible. To get into the flat, the Germans would have to break down the door.

The retrieved items found shelter in a hiding place under the cellar stairs in the Płachtowskis' flat. I also took from our flat a pile of Father's letters sent from different prisoner-of-war camps and put them in the pocket of a borrowed coat I was wearing. The next morning, I learned that the letters had been found in the streets. The pocket must have had a hole in it; as we were crossing the roof on our way back, the bundle fell out and the wind scattered the letters all over Żolibórz.

Another memorable event of the period was the *Kedyw* operation of 12 February 1944. We received an order to execute Ernest Dürfeld, the German director of the Warsaw gasworks and power station. He had been working closely with the Gestapo since 1940, and was held responsible for many arrests and deportations of Poles employed by the two establishments. The Underground Court, acting in the name of the Home Army of the Republic of Poland, condemned him to death.

Every morning, escorted by a German policeman, Dürfeld would drive along Bracka Street to Jerusalem Avenue. We studied the route carefully and worked out a simple plan of action. First, Antek and Columbus would throw a *filipinka*, a grenade designed to explode on impact, at the moving car. Once the car stopped, Stasinek and I, waiting in a doorway some 200 metres down the road, would complete the job. Unfortunately, Stasinek left me on my own, having gone to check whether everything was in order with the other two. I was armed with a Thompson sub-machine gun, hidden under my coat. The gun had come from a recent parachute drop and this was the first time I was to use it.

Dürfeld's car arrived. The grenade thrown by the others landed, I think, somewhere near the car. I didn't see the point of impact. The car came to a stop just across the street from me. I started shooting but, after the first series, the Thompson jammed. The passengers of the car took cover in a nearby building, while the uniformed policeman hid behind the car. I had a grenade in my pocket and should have thrown it, but I missed the chance; I was left on my own, my gun had jammed, and my mind went blank. All I wanted at that moment was to join my friends and be out of there, at any price. I left the doorway and started running towards our getaway car. The German policeman saw me and opened fire. I'll cop it this time, I thought, as I sprinted round the corner to our car. In an instant we were in and, with screeching tyres, on our way. We had survived, but so had Dürfeld. To this day, the forgotten grenade is one of the greatest regrets of my life. Back in our hideout, I discovered sharp fragments of stucco embedded in my hat; the policeman had aimed too high and his bullets had splintered the wall above my head. I had been lucky. Another attempt at the execution, organised by a different unit, also failed. There were casualties. I have often wondered whether Dürfeld lived out his years at home in Germany, in peace. I shall never know.

TWELVE

The Most Elegant of *Kedyw*'s Operations

One of the most difficult and successful operations undertaken by *Kedyw* took place on 4 March 1944. A German railway policeman, Schmaltz, was condemned to death by the Home Army Court. This man, whose pretty and feminine looks had earned him the nickname of *Panienka*, or 'Miss', was particularly bloodthirsty, and known for his cruelty. Disguised as a girl, he would creep up on children and women stealing bits of coal from stationary railway wagons and shoot them on the spot. He had killed over a hundred people in this way. Several earlier attempts at his execution had failed. Schmaltz knew that his life was in danger, and except for his murderous forays he hardly ever left the railway guards' lodgings. This building, which stood in the middle of tracks between the Central and Western railway stations, housed some ten railway guards with *Panienka* in command. The main barracks of the German police force at Narutowicz Square were about two kilometres away. Polish railwaymen had provided us with plans of the guards' premises. The house was completely surrounded with barbed wire. We had to work out a stratagem to enter the precinct and carry out the death sentence without incurring casualties.

We prepared the operation with great care. In addition to the policeman's uniform which we already possessed – I had used it on many occasions – we needed a soldier's uniform. With our fingers crossed, in a stolen German car, we drove past the German army barracks in Powązki. Our driver was Antek and the team included Janek, Stasinek and myself. Only Janek could speak German. He wore an SS officer's tunic, riding boots and trousers; the latter were not quite the right hue, but as only the top part of his body appeared in the car window, this was not important. Just as we were passing the guard box of the barracks, the engine stalled. Janek got out of the car and, as the Citroën bonnet opened up in two halves to the sides, half hidden between them he tried to restart the engine. At any moment the barracks guards or even a passing *Wehrmacht* soldier was likely to offer help. Janek's German could not possibly pass for that of an SS officer.

Suddenly, a German soldier approached the car. He saluted, clicked his heels, stood to attention and asked for a lift: he had been out on a pass and feared he would be late. Janek did not bother to look up. '*Raus,*' he barked, and the disappointed soldier clicked his heels again, saluted: '*Jawohl Herr Stürmführer,*' did a regulation about turn and walked away. At last the engine fired. We were off.

Three hundred metres down the road, there was our *Wehrmacht* soldier again. He stood to attention. Saluted. Could we give him a lift? This time we were in a more generous mood. I got out to make room for him in the middle. He sat down, his rifle between his knees. 'Your rifle,' I asked him politely, stretching out my hand. I was dressed in a black oilcloth coat of the type favoured by the Gestapo plainclothes men. He was rather surprised, but handed the gun over. We were on our way.

Janek turned to the German. 'We are Polish Army soldiers. We will not hurt you. We kill only SS men, not *Werhmacht* soldiers.'

Never before or since have I seen a man more startled. Two or three kilometres down the road, we stopped in a small wood. 'Take your uniform off.' We took his uniform and boots, leaving him in his vest and underpants. It was January. There was snow on the ground. I would like to have been a fly on the wall on his return to barracks, and to have heard his report! Now we had both uniforms needed for the operation.

The plan was that Columbus, disguised as a German policeman, and Janek, dressed as a German soldier, would pretend to have caught a Polish thief, this part to be played by Antek in the garb of a Polish worker, which was Antek's favoured attire anyway. With their sub-machine guns at the ready, they would escort the man to the main entrance of the guards' house, to entrust him to the tender mercies of Commander Schmaltz, or *Panienka*. The rest of us, numbering about fourteen, would meanwhile take over the builders' yard backing onto the railway tracks. This task completed, Kazik's team of five or six, including Stasinek and myself, would get through a gap in the wooden fence of the yard and run to the barbed wire surrounding the guards' house. The wire cut – procuring the necessary wire cutters had been a bit of a problem – we would enter the guards' house by the back door.

We carried out the plan point by point. A covered lorry took us

Portrait of Tadeusz Likiernik, the author's father, painted by a fellow prisoner of war.

Wanda Likiernik, the author's mother.

The author's school identity card.

TOP: The author's mother with the author in 1934;
Janek Srebrny in the middle, Roman Mularczyk
(later known as Bratny) on the right.

ABOVE: The author in 1939, in the uniform of
school cadets.

The author in his early twenties.

The author in Sopot in
October 1945.

Olek Tyrawski in the uniform of school cadets, summer 1939.

St John's Cathedral after
the Warsaw Rising.

City centre, Warsaw.

TOP: View of the Old City, at the start of the Warsaw Rising.

ABOVE: Nowy Świat Street, near the Sacred Cross Church.

TOP: The insurgents, city centre.

ABOVE: Freta Street, after the Warsaw Rising.

straight into the builders' yard. We mustered the yard's employees in one place and kept an eye on them. Making a hole in the fence didn't take more than a few minutes, and the planks left in place made it invisible from the guards' house.

We didn't have to wait long before we saw Columbus and Janek escorting the supposed thief along the tracks towards the guards' house. They helped him along with shoves and kicks; unnecessarily realistic, as Antek later complained. As they were entering the guards' house, we cut the wire and rushed in. Suddenly, a guard's uniform blocked my field of vision. Point blank, I let my *Parabellum* go. The man fell and the view cleared. We ran into the main hall. There, with his back to us was *Panienka*, taking charge of the 'thief'. Columbus and Janek, with their sub-machine guns constantly at the ready, opened fire, killing *Panienka* and the other guards in sight. A man in civilian clothes begged for his life, assuring us that he happened to be there by accident. Alas, we let him go. The guards' house was ours.

We captured a heavy machinegun, some twenty rifles and several pistols. With a bunch of rifles on my back, I ran towards our lorry which in the meantime had pulled up to the hole in the wooden fence. I heard the joyous shouts of passengers from a passing train; they'd had a grandstand view and had no doubts as to what was happening.

German police could close on us at any time. But superstitiously, not to tempt fate, we had not made detailed plans for our return journey. We climbed under the tarpaulin and drove towards Żolibórz to disperse in the area. But first we had to secure the captured weapons. We stopped a horse-drawn cart loaded with firewood, hid our booty under the wood and took it to Mrs Gurda, Mundek's widow. In spite of the risk, she agreed to hide the unexpected arsenal in her cellar for a few days, giving us time to find a more permanent cache. The operation being a success we went later that day to a double celebration at Kazik's, our victory and his name-day, which happened to be on 4 March.

However, disaster struck several days later, when in a tram Kazik ran into the civilian whom we had spared. The man recognised him and alerted the Germans. Kazik and his wife were taken to the Gestapo headquarters. Under interrogation, he did not give away a single name to his torturers. At the time of their arrest, Zosia Czechowska, our courier, happened to be in the house. While the Gestapo were busy searching the apartment, Zosia, unnoticed, dashed inside, picked up Kazik's son, a baby of several months, and left unobserved. As she could have come from one of the other flats in the building, the guard posted at the entrance did not stop her. As soon as she left, the Germans went looking for the baby. With the child in their hands they could have made the parents talk by threatening to kill or maim him. But luckily Zosia got him out in time, thus saving the little boy. He is now a middle-aged man and lives in the USA. By chance, I met him and his American wife recently, on a visit to Warsaw.

THIRTEEN

A Busy Day

I DO NOT RECALL ALL OF THE ACTIONS carried out between the execution of *Panienka* on 4 March and *Kedyw*'s last job before the start of the open warfare of the Warsaw Rising. The date of 15 June was the day of the 'Gestapo Hunt'. All the sabotage units in Warsaw had been mobilised to ambush and attack all motorcars with registration numbers beginning with POL 47, a distinguishing mark of the Warsaw Gestapo force. The 'hunt' was to last only from 11 a.m. to 12 noon, but during that single hour, in a dozen selected places round the city, the Gestapo were to pay in kind for the deaths of a group of 100 Pawiak prison inmates recently executed in the streets of the capital.

For us this busy day started at 10 a.m., when Janusz and I left the house and walked in the direction of the Vistula riverside park. The streets were almost empty. I carried a small suitcase with a spare sub-machine gun and had my own concealed under my coat, its strap as usual round my neck. Antoni and Janek waited for us with the car. By that time the Germans had managed to reduce considerably the number of hideouts available to us and, in order not to attract the attention of nosy neighbours, we had to restrict our daily comings and goings. One way was to cram several jobs into a single twenty-four-hour period and thus, in addition to the attack on the Gestapo motorcars, our schedule for the day included reconnoitring at the site of a planned attack on a train carrying Polish slave-labourers to Germany, a thirty-kilometre trip out of town. Furthermore, at 4 p.m. we were supposed to be back in Warsaw to meet a fellow conspirator working in *Arbeitsamt*, the Labour Office. He was to confirm that Bock, another German official condemned to death by the Underground, was working in his office that day. Bock was in the habit of leaving the building at about 6 p.m. Immediately after getting confirmation, or between 4 p.m. and 6 p.m., we were supposed to drop off Janusz in Żolibórz and collect Stefan, who knew the condemned German by sight.

At the time, the streets of Warsaw and the roads to and from the capital were crawling with German patrols. Pedestrians and cars were being frequently stopped for document checks. Just as well that some of our extensive schedule involving a lot of driving and therefore very risky, had to be abandoned before completion. However, even for the hardened conspirators that we were, the 'hunt' itself and the out of town trip were interesting enough to warrant reporting.

On the morning in question there were four of us in the car, each with a sub-machine gun in his lap concealed under a raincoat. Our first ambush was set up in a wide street which led from the Pawiak prison, through the ruins of the ghetto, straight to the Gestapo headquarters. Some cars with the POL 47 registration number were bound to use this route. Janusz and Janek, both of whom were to die a couple of months later in the Warsaw Rising, took their positions in the street some fifty metres ahead of our car in the direction from which we expected the Gestapo to come. Each had one of our home-made impact grenades in his pocket. Antoni and I were to open fire on the car immobilised by the explosions.

The next minute Columbus, who was supposed to join us on foot, suddenly appeared by our car: 'The military police,' he said hurriedly, short of breath, opening the door of our vehicle. 'Scram! Three lorries teeming with them are coming down the next street, only 200 metres away. Scarper!' he repeated. Five of us clambered into our stolen Opel and we sped away in the direction of Żolibórz.

At 11.30 a.m. we reached the Gdańsk station viaduct, where we set up another ambush. There was still half an hour of the 'hunt' to go. But this time providence must have been on the side of the enemy, as not a single target car appeared. And at noon we had to leave. In normal times our next trip, to the Piaseczno forest, could have been a very pleasant outing, but times were not normal and running into a German road block or patrol was not a picnic. Much depended on the experience of the driver. Fortunately, the road was free of blocks and we were able to reconnoitre at the area of the planned action as ordered.

At 4 p.m. Kostek, our friend in the *Arbeitsamt*, confirmed that Bock was in the office. 'Come here at 5 p.m. I'll keep an eye on him for you,' he volunteered. We drove back to Żolibórz – another anxious hour driving round the streets of Warsaw. By then the day seemed to be growing excessively long. Stefan, who was waiting for us, leapt into the car before it came to a stop. Back to the centre. But it just wasn't our day. Luck continued to be on the side of the enemy: the German, Bock, had left half an hour earlier than usual. Crestfallen, we had to turn back. We had been denied our prey. We had risked our lives for nothing. Tired and dispirited, we drove down the boulevard along the Vistula.

Back in Żoliborz, Antoni suddenly shouted 'Gestapo!' And indeed, an empty POL 47 motorcar was parked at the kerb outside the house at 5 Krasiński Street. We knew that several days earlier the inhabitants of the house, the entire Przywecki family, had been arrested; they would all die in Auschwitz. Janek was in command that day. 'To work?' he asked curtly.

'Yes!' came the unanimous reply. It was now well past noon, so past the time of the designated 'hunt'. But who cared? We could always report that the Germans attacked us first. Quite simple, really. (Many years later, in Warsaw, Hania Rybicka, daughter of the commanding officer of the *Kedyw* Warsaw District, showed me our report with the slightly adjusted version of events, and it wasn't until 1992 that I let her have the true account.)

We concocted our plan of action in minutes. We assumed that the Gestapo car would follow Krasiński street to the Vistula Boulevard. We left our car in the Boulevard, round the corner, invisible from Krasinski Street. Antoni and I took position behind a small earth bank, no more than one metre high, just round the corner from the Gestapo car. Janek and Stefan hid in a Krasiński Street garden between us and the car. When the targets reached their position, they were to throw an impact grenade and fire at the occupants. Antoni and I were, if necessary, to complete the job with our machine guns and to grab any German weapons. A rather worrying aspect of the plan was that the area was probably crawling with German cars, while our cover was far from adequate. But we made our decision: we would attack.

Ten, fifteen minutes went by . . . and suddenly we were in business. The Gestapo car moved off from the kerb. Janek threw the grenade. It exploded, but caused no obvious damage. The car came to a halt some sixty metres from our position. The Gestapo men scrambled out. One ran across the street. Antoni and I opened fire. He fell. The other two dropped to the pavement and returned fire. Small hillocks of soil erupted next to me. 'Antoni is aiming too low', I thought. Only later did it occur to me that they were German bullets. Janek and Stefan were nowhere to be seen. After a short exchange of fire, Antoni shouted 'To the car!' We leapt in and turned around, driving in the direction of the city centre. A few hundred metres down the road, there was a small island with a large tree in the middle. Antoni veered round it, shouting 'Get ready to shoot!' He wound down his window. Having evidently assumed that this was the end of the incident, the two Gestapo men were up again. They looked unhurt. Antoni stepped on the accelerator. The car sped along the left side of the street near the kerb. With his left hand on the driving wheel and his gun in the other, Antoni started shooting through his window. I was ready to shoot from the back seat, but there was no way to open the side window. I fired close to the glass. The bullets went through leaving holes in the glass, but the rest of it shattered and turned opaque. I shot through the back window. The same happened. My magazine was empty. I looked at Antoni. He was still driving fast, steering with only one hand, dodging the German cars attracted by the noise of the fusillade. His right hand was bleeding badly.

We owed our lives to the total surprise. The German machine guns could have made mincemeat of us. But we gave them no time to start. We could not risk driving for long with shattered windows. Doubling back, we drove about one-and-a-half kilometres to Wilson Square and abandoned the car. We decided to go on foot to a hideout in lower Żolibórz. I was carrying two exposed sub-machine guns, having no means to cover them, so I stopped a passer-by and 'borrowed' his raincoat. Antoni needed medical attention; he was getting weaker by the minute. Only then did I understand what had happened. A German bullet had hit his gun's magazine, which exploded in his hand. His right hand was badly shattered, part of it gone. Halfway to our hideout Antoni stopped. 'I am done in,' he said. 'My cousin lives here, he will shelter me and call a doctor.' I was left alone with two sub-machine guns and no ammunition. I had to stay off the streets and, whenever possible, kept to the allotments. But these were fenced off with barbed wire which ripped open the back of my jacket. Going to the Płachtowski's in this state risked blowing a safe house. Nor could I risk being seen in my local streets or anywhere near the area of the shoot-out.

I decided to while away an hour or two in the garden of a villa and then phone to summon a friend with a coat and a bag for the weapons. I tried the gate in the wire netting of one of the gardens. It was locked. I pressed the bell. A little girl came out of the house but took fright and, instead of opening the gate, ran back to the house, screaming at the top of her voice. A little further along the fence there was another small gate. I pushed it, it gave way. I dashed across the garden and down some steps into a cellar. I dropped the guns, wrapped in the coat, and took off my torn jacket. With the folded jacket under my arm, I returned to the street and walked calmly but quickly to Olek's house. Luckily, he and his wife lived nearby; they gave me a raincoat and a suitcase. I retraced my steps to the villa to retrieve the guns. To my surprise, the house was guarded by 'the blues' (Polish police) and the street around it was crowded with onlookers.

'What's happening here?' I asked.

The gist of the garbled answers was that a little girl had seen a bandit carry a dead baby in his arms and deposit it in the cellar. At that moment a couple of policemen appeared on the cellar steps. One carried a bundle wrapped in a coat. The girl must have seen Antoni's blood stains on the coat and hence the mistake and the panic.

Suddenly, from being simply dangerous, the situation became alarming. Antoni was wounded, the other two had disappeared without trace and two sub-machine guns were lost through my fault. Weapons were precious; we were expected to capture them from the Gestapo, not hand them back to the enemy. All due to one unauthorised operation. Fortunately, I knew the officer in charge of the Żolibórz police station, a good Pole with connections to the Underground. I ran to the police station only to be told that the man was resting at home with a fractured leg. I hastened to his house. 'Leave it to me,' he said. 'I shall deal with it. Come back tomorrow.'

And indeed, the next day the two sub-machine guns were returned to me; 'the blues' could easily have sold them, they were worth a fortune on the black market. The Polish police filed a report on the death of a baby in a bandit attack, a matter of no interest to the Germans.

I found out later what happened to Stefan and Janek. Having realised that their grenade had missed the target, they tried to escape through the gardens of Kaniowska Street. The Germans spotted them and opened fire. Stefan was killed, but Janek managed to get away.

When it came to the official report, uncertain of our headquarters' reaction, we kept to the story of an unprovoked German attack – and we were heartily congratulated. Unknowingly, we had killed Jung and Hoffman, two Gestapo agents who had been condemned to death by the Home Army, but attempts on whom had so far failed. Regrettably, poor Stefan, who only joined us at 4 p.m., was dead by 6 p.m.

FOURTEEN

The Arrest of Wacek and his Mother.
Ghetto Rising and its Liquidation

WACEK KOC HAD BEEN MY FRIEND WELL BEFORE THE WAR, as far back as the first form of *gimnazjum*. I have referred in previous chapters to his family and to his mother's hospitable home. From the start of the German occupation Wacek worked for the Underground, and also helped me into it. But then, as it happened, we went our separate ways in the clandestine activity, I in *Kedyw* and he in Intelligence. Until April 1943 he was in Warsaw, being later transferred to Lwów in the Ukraine. His chief, Colonel Pohowski, a mysterious personage, made great demands on Wacek. One was to become fluent in languages, especially German and Russian. This achieved, Wacek was sent to the east.

His departure coincided with the Warsaw Ghetto Rising. I remember that day vividly. Because of the outbreak of fighting between the Jewish insurgents and the Germans, the Żolibórz tram stopped short of the ghetto and we had to continue on foot to the Old City; we parted there and Wacek walked on, all the way to the station in the centre. In those days any separation had the seeds of finality about it. With Wacek gone, I continued to see his mother and his sister, Jaga. They lived only a few blocks away from us. There was little news from Wacek after that.

On 8 May 1943, my name-day, I held a small party in our flat. The guests included Olek Tyrawski, Renia Wiączek, Zosia Czechowska and Elżka Majkowska. We danced and listened to records brought by Jaga from her absent father's collection. Next day, about 10 a.m., I took them back. Fela, the housekeeper, opened the door. Jaga was out. 'Just leave the records,' called Mrs Koc through the bathroom door. 'She won't be back till the afternoon.' I left. Mr Balcerzak, my workmate from Pfeiffer's, who ran a small clandestine tannery in the basement of the house, saw me going. He told me later that hardly had I gone out of the door when a Gestapo car pulled up in front of the house. I had just turned the corner and did not see anything. My luck had held; the Germans didn't see me leaving either, or they would have pulled me in as well.

The Gestapo were still searching Mrs Koc's flat when her seventeen-year-old younger son, Andrzej, returned home. As he was climbing the stairs his mother, having recognised his steps, dashed to the door shouting: 'Gestapo! Run! Run!' Before the Germans managed to drag her away from the door, Andrzej had fled. He survived then only to be killed over a year later, in the Warsaw Rising. Mrs Koc and her housekeeper were arrested, savagely beaten and deported to Auschwitz where they both died.

Not only Jews died in Auschwitz . . .

Some time before that, Wacek had been arrested in Lwów. The Germans had set up a trap in a previously safe house and he just walked into it. He was first imprisoned under terrible conditions in Lwów and after three months moved to Buchenwald, another notorious German concentration camp near Weimar.

I met Wacek again in 1945. Miraculously, we had both survived the war.

From 1942, Jews were being deported in increasing numbers to Auschwitz and Treblinka. *Umschlagplatz*, the site of entraining, was a few hundred metres from the Gdańsk railway station and about two kilometres from my house, as the crow flies. The grossly over-loaded locked cattle wagons with their tightly packed human cargo were kept, sometimes for several days, in the sidings without food or water. The groans, the wailing, the heart-rending cries carried far in the night from these death-bound trains. I was able to watch them from the viaduct above the sidings. The wagons were locked at all times and all one could see were hands clutching the bars of the tiny windows, and the eyes behind the bars. '*Wasser, wasser*, water, water!' were the abject pleas. German soldiers were posted every twenty metres along the track. I saw one of them fill a bucket from a tap. He carried it towards a wagon and then, in view of all, he emptied its contents on the ground. To this day I shake with rage at the memory.

But not all Jews were prepared to die as helpless victims, and preparations had been made for a rising. By then the deportations to death camps had reduced the Jewish population to about twenty or

---

¹ Soviet political police, later called KGB.

thirty thousand. The ghetto erupted in April 1943. It was immediately surrounded by the German police with Lithuanian, Ukrainian and Latvian auxiliaries. Helping the insurgents was a near impossible task. Our Warsaw unit of *Kedyw* was ordered to attack the advancing German troops. We killed one policeman, we threw a grenade at a patrol moving into attack. Weapons and ammunition were smuggled in for the insurgents, but inevitably in insufficient amounts. The Home Army's arsenal wasn't large enough even for its own later rising of 1 August 1944. *Kedyw*, somewhat better armed, was an exception. The accusations levelled at the Polish Underground of not helping the ghetto insurgents cannot be justified. Forewarned by the Underground's emissary Jan Karski, and by the Polish Government in London, neither Churchill nor Roosevelt did anything to prevent the disaster. They did not respond in any way, and their power and potential were infinitely greater than ours.

The ghetto burned for many days. The Germans were setting fire to it house by house. To save the rest of the city, the volunteer firemen of Warsaw, including my friend Janusz, kept hosing down the roofs on the outer side of the ghetto wall. He shared with us later the macabre scenes he had witnessed in the process. The Germans destroyed the entire ghetto; an area equivalent to that of a largish town had been reduced to rubble and cinders.

In 1944 only two buildings remained standing there, the Grzybów church and the infamous Pawiak prison with its Polish inmates – from among these the Germans used to select Polish hostages to be murdered in reprisals: a hundred Poles were shot each time a German was killed in the streets of Warsaw. Thus perished Stach, Zosia's brother. Red posters with the names of selected hostages would be regularly displayed throughout the town: a hundred names of those already shot and another hundred chosen for the next execution. During one such execution I happened to be no further than 300 metres from where it was taking place in the Gdańsk railway station. There was a short burst of machine-gun fire. There would be five bodies, I knew it. Then silence. The next group of condemned men loaded the corpses on to a lorry. Another series . . . and another . . . Invariably one had friends in the Pawiak prison and inevitably, sooner or later, some of them were among those murdered. I thanked God that I was part of the Underground and from time to time had the chance to take revenge, to fight the barbarians. Total impotence would have been difficult to bear. Polish women used to place flowers and light candles at the sites of execution. Once, in the centre of Warsaw, a German patrol sprayed them with machine-gun fire, leaving many dead and wounded.

Another momentous event of 1943 was *Katyń*. On 5 April the graves of 4,000 Polish officers were discovered in the *Katyń* forest near Smolensk. They had been murdered in 1940, well before the German invasion of the USSR in June 1941, and thus at a time when the territory was in Soviet hands. The massacre had been carried out by the NKVD[1] with a bullet in the back of the head, a method favoured by that organisation. Stalin denied all responsibility and shifted the blame on to the Germans. In the autumn of 1941, still unaware of this crime, the Polish Government in exile in London, headed by General Sikorski, concluded a treaty with the USSR, by then a member of the anti-German coalition. This led to the release of Polish prisoners-of-war and others held in Soviet camps and prisons, and to the formation of the Polish Army in the USSR.

In September 1939 when Stalin and Hitler, working in close partnership, divided Poland between them, some 30,000 Polish officers had fallen into Soviet hands. Now, only a fraction of that number rallied to the colours. At least 15,000 officers were missing. The *Katyń* graves provided a partial explanation (sites of other massacres were still to be discovered). The Polish Government's request to the International Red Cross for an independent inquiry was used by Stalin as a pretext to sever diplomatic relations with the Polish Government in London. He tried to pass off the murders as a German atrocity, and any questioning of his veracity was rejected by him as an unacceptable affront.

In 1992 the actual order for the execution of 24,000 Polish officers, policemen and civil servants did come to light. It had been signed by Stalin, Molotov, Gromyko and other members of the Soviet Politburo. At the time in question, however, the perpetrators of the massacre, ostensibly offended by having their sincerity questioned, and in preparation for their subsequent conquest of Eastern and Central Europe, severed diplomatic relations with the government representing the victims. The cynicism and the perfidy of the act beggar belief. The allies, mainly the USA and Great Britain, their leaders in full possession of the facts, failed to side with Poland. They needed Stalin and his army on the eastern front and did not wish to jeopardise the alliance. Soon after, General Sikorski, the head of the Polish Government in London, died in an air accident in Gibraltar. The cause of the accident has remained unexplained to this day.

In the meantime, the Red Army continued its progress

westwards and on 4 January 1944 crossed the pre-war Polish border. Soldiers of the Underground loyal to the Polish Government in London fought side by side with it in taking Wilno and Lwów, both Polish cities before the war. In recognition of their help, they were invited to a victory banquet. Towards its end the building was surrounded by NKVD troops, and all the members of the Polish Home Army were arrested and deported into the depths of the Soviet Union (only a few survivors returned to Poland in 1956, three years after Stalin's death and at the time of the temporary relaxation of the communist rule, initiated by Krushchev). Stalin's aim had been to retain the Polish territories east of the River Bug, first acquired in 1939 at the time of his alliance with Hitler. The Polish patriots were in the way.

FIFTEEN

July 1944: Red Army at the Gates of Warsaw

By JULY 1944 THE FRONT was rapidly approaching Warsaw. The inhabitants of the city watched the retreating German troops and their Hungarian toadies. Not without *Schadenfreude*. Yesterday's conquerors presented a sorry sight now. There was no hint of the arrogance and haughtiness so blatant in 1939 at the time of their invasion of Poland, and again in 1941 when they were preparing to attack the USSR. The Warsaw sky became the scene of repeated dogfights between German and Soviet planes. In short, it became obvious that the end of German rule in Warsaw was in sight.

On either 25 or 26 July, cycling along a Żolibórz street, I came upon a bunch of weary-looking Hungarians in horse-drawn carts. As their officer stopped pacing the pavement, I went up to him. '*Deutschland kaputt*,' I said with a smile, mindful of the old Polish-Hungarian brotherhood. His roar of '*What did you say? How dare you?*' in response showed none of the brotherly feelings expected. His hand shot down to his holster. I just leapt on my bike and pedalled as fast as I could. He was definitely not a good Hungarian.

In our unit of *Kedyw*, the chances of a successful rising against the Germans were not highly rated. Stasinek and Olszyna were staunchly pessimistic. We knew only too well that, while *Kedyw* possessed some light weapons, other units were short of arms and especially of anti-tank weapons. Our Home Army, with roughly one grenade per five soldiers, had to face an enemy still armed to the teeth.

My friend Roman Mularczyk (later known as Roman Bratny, the celebrated writer) came to see me several days before the Rising. 'Mark my words,' he said. 'The Russians will provoke an insurrection in Warsaw and when we start fighting, they'll stop their advance and let the Germans finish us off.'

'If you and I know that,' I replied, 'so must our leaders. I don't believe that an order to start a general rising would be given without the prior approval of the British and the Soviets.'

An open insurrection against the incomparably better-armed German troops could make sense only with the certainty of immediate help and material support from the allies. At the time we were unaware of the Soviet treachery in Wilno, but our leaders must have known about it. If they had ever had any confidence in the Soviet ally, that event must have shattered it. Yet in the opinion of General Bór-Komorowski, the commander of the Home Army, expressed in his memoirs, liberated Warsaw would have offered a bridgehead which Stalin could not afford to ignore. But as events proved he did, because it suited his wider plans. The general must have forgotten that millions of their own citizens had been murdered without qualms on the orders of the Soviet leader. The destruction of the Polish capital and the death of its defenders was also part of Stalin's schemes. By allowing the Nazis to eliminate Polish patriots, he could avoid doing the dirty work himself. Great Britain was too far to offer the insurgents any effective help, but in the event, she actually vetoed the use of the Polish Parachute Brigade in support of the fighting in Warsaw. The Brigade, stationed in Great Britain, happened to be commanded by General Sosabowski, Stasinek's father.

SIXTEEN

The Warsaw Rising I
(1 August 1944)

THE ENTIRE WARSAW UNDERGROUND FORCE was put on full alert. The General Rising was scheduled to start at 5 p.m. on 1 August 1944. We received our orders on 31 July and Home Army detachments assembled at their designated points. The first objective of *Kedyw* were the German Army stores in Stawki. These, we knew, contained food and uniforms but no weapons. We, in *Kedyw*, were relatively well armed with captured weapons and a few Thompson guns from parachute drops. We were also battle-hardened. According to the plan, having secured the stores, we were to march to the PKO building in the city centre and place ourselves at the disposal of General Monter, the commander of the Rising. The battle order stipulated that once the capital had been liberated we were to return to our jump-off points, secure all weapons in arms caches and remain prepared for possible further clandestine activity under Soviet occupation.

I wasn't too excited about this last part of the plan. In my mind's eye I saw a victory parade, with weapons, in full glory. I was only twenty-one, and after years of nerve-racking clandestine work I hoped for some recognition. We were owed acknowledgement, we were overdue for celebrations, and were full of hope that our equally patriotic girls would recognise our valour and succumb to the charms of the uniform. But how different reality turned out to be!

On 1 August, on leaving our base, I saw my old friend Olek Tyrawski at the head of his platoon. There was no time to talk and we just waved to one another. Several minutes later, about 3 p.m., as they were crossing Mickiewicz Street, a German tank opened fire and Olek was hit in the forehead. He died instantly. He may have been the first casualty of the insurrection. I only learned about his death ten days later.

In a covered lorry driven by Columbus, our Żolibórz detachment of *Kedyw* reached our jump-off point in the grounds of a school bordering on the Stawki stores. There we joined forces with the Mokotów and Wola detachments of the Warsaw *Kedyw*. The operation has since been commemorated by a bronze plaque on the wall of the school; the *Umschlagplatz* monument has been erected next to it.

We seized the school at 3.30 p.m. Columbus and I went to move our lorry to a safer location. We travelled maybe ten metres when an artillery shell exploded at the very place we had just vacated. Our first artillery shell had fortunately missed us.

Our attack on the German stores evolved according to plan. At exactly 5 p.m. we jumped over the fence at the back of the large area, at least a hectare, occupied by the stores. The main building was guarded by a small SS unit. We shot dead several of the men and took the stores very quickly. The two Krauts who tried to escape into the ruins of the ghetto on the other side of the stores area were also killed. Suddenly, inside the stores, a group of about fifty men ran towards us. They wore the striped garb of concentration camp prisoners. They called out to us, but we couldn't understand a single word. They were Greek Jews from Salonika who had been put to work in the stores. With difficulty, we explained to them what was happening and that they were now free. This act of liberation of foreigner prisoners is also commemorated on the bronze plaque.

A young SS officer who survived our initial assault had built a barricade of packing cases in the big hall on the first floor. He must have amassed a large amount of ammunition, as he kept the main door under almost constant fire. Columbus was wounded in the hand. But just next to the officer's hideout we spied another door and decided to blow it up. Antek did it with an impact grenade. In his hate-fired eagerness, he did not take cover in time and his legs stopped a number of fragments. After Columbus, he was our second casualty.

As I learned after the war, the inhabitants of the Old Town later managed to remove tons of provisions from the stores: flour, sugar, cereals etc. They carried the bags and boxes on their backs. These supplies helped them to survive the next three weeks of savage fighting, when the Old Town was completely cut off from the outside world.

We spent the night in the stores. We found a large stock of

panterki, camouflage jackets used by German paratroopers, and, naturally, we put them on. As many of us had joined the Rising in civvies, it was only now that we began to look like a military unit. I was wearing a pair of smart high boots and a Polish officer tunic given to me by Janusz's mother. The newly acquired camouflage jacket went over my tunic; I was very proud of my uniform.

A month later these captured jackets came in very handy; they probably saved our lives.

As the east-west route was cut off by the Germans protecting the bridge over the Vistula, we were not able to report to General Monter in the city centre. Instead, Colonel Radosław, the area commander, ordered us to Wola. Antek, who couldn't walk, and Columbus, with his wounded hand, became our joint drivers and took charge of our lorry. Antek, wounded in both legs, operated the driving wheel and the gears, while Columbus had his feet on the pedals. They drove first along Okopowa Street. Then I saw them turning right. Suddenly, they were reversing back towards us at great speed. They had found the street barred by a German tank some 300 metres ahead. It was only their presence of mind and well coordinated driving that saved them; they managed to back out of the street before the Germans opened fire. Later, together with a unit of the *Zośka* battalion, we captured that tank. Repaired by Columbus, it served us for several days.

On our march to Wola we passed the Pfeiffer tannery, where I had worked for a year in 1943. The tanners were prevented from leaving the building by the sudden outbreak of fighting. They greeted us, their re-born Army, with enthusiasm. Our detachment of about a hundred, all dressed in the captured camouflage jackets, must have been a heart-warming sight. Stasinek headed the unit and I marched next to him, a Thompson gun under my arm. My former workmates recognised me and hails and hurras, shouts of 'Stach, Bravo!', followed us for a while. I was feeling proud and happy, for the first and only time in the two months of the Rising.

On arriving in Wola, we found a suitable garden and marked an area for parachute drops with white sheets. We were full of hope, aid was bound to arrive any time now: weapons, ammunition, all that was required for the conduct of war. But in vain did we search the sky. It rained a little that day, the only time that the sky over Warsaw was overcast during those two momentous months. Later in the day, Colonel Radosław sent me on patrol. I was to reconnoitre the German police barracks in St Zofia's Hospital and the surrounding area. I went with two men. My report to Radosław on our return was laconic: the building was still in German hands. This was my only contact with Radosław during the Rising; I still remember how impressed I was by his uniform of a cloak and helmet. In the evening, General Bór-Komorowski, the CO of the Home Army, arrived in Wola for an inspection.

The next day, Radosław ordered Stasinek to take the German police barracks. Once more we followed him through the streets of Wola. The local people greeted us with enthusiasm. Their cheers followed us all the way. Men and women ran into the streets with bread, sweetmeats, whatever they could lay their hands on – it was very moving. Especially with hindsight: several days later the same people were slaughtered en masse by the Germans.

On 4 August Stasinek, Jerzy Kaczyński, our doctor, and I climbed to the third floor of the house adjoining the hospital building to assess the situation and in particular to have a good look at the yard we would have to cross on the way to the hospital. Stasinek, as usual brave to a fault, looked out of the window. Hardly had I finished saying: 'Take care. Don't stick your head out,' when I heard a dull gunshot report and Stasinek fell back with blood covering his face. 'I can't see, I can't see!' he cried. The wound was light, but it affected his good eye. Stasinek had sight in one eye only, having lost the other in a childhood accident. Now his good eye was gone. He had to be evacuated and joined Antek in the Karolkowa Street hospital. Janek took over command.

The hospital building was surrounded by a brick wall. We decided to attack from Żelazna Street. The distance from the wall to the hospital entrance was some twenty to thirty metres. First we tried to set fire to the building next door, hoping that it would spread to the barracks. I threw a petrol bottle at the ground floor, but the fire did not spread to the remaining levels. About 7 p.m. it was beginning to get dark and it was time to attack. We blew up part of the wall and dashed through the breach. Just at that moment somebody in the crowd of enthusiastic onlookers started playing a lively tune on an accordion. Full of ardour we advanced: at last a straight fight, face-to-face. The huge entrance door wouldn't yield. As we were forcing it, there was a loud explosion and something like a club hit me in the back. I felt no real pain. 'What was that?' I asked the man next to me. 'Something thumped me.'

He looked. 'You are bleeding,' he said. 'They dropped a grenade from the top window. Off with you to the dressing station.'

Leaving him my sub-machine gun and my *Parabellum*, I ran back across the yard to our nurses. I was dizzy. A loud noise reverberated inside my head. Was it the explosion? The girls put me on a stretcher and examined me. There were grenade splinters embedded at the top and in the middle of my back, in my right arm and right thigh. I couldn't walk any more. I had to go to hospital, where I hoped to join Antek and Stasinek.

What I didn't know was that the Karolkowa Street hospital had already fallen to the Ukrainian SS volunteers, German auxiliaries, and that they had already shot the wounded, including Antek, in cold blood, in their beds. Stasinek only escaped this fate as his wife, one of the nurses, got him out in the nick of time and both of them managed to get away.

I was taken to another makeshift hospital in the Appeal Court building in Leszno Street. I was left on the stretcher for an hour waiting for a surgeon. I shall never forget what followed. First, he started pulling out the shrapnel. Without anaesthetic. These fragments were well embedded, like fish hooks, in my back, arm and thigh. By then they had almost become part of me. Suddenly, he had a flash of inspiration: he soaked a strip of gauze in alcohol and pushed it right through the flesh of my thigh, from one side to the other; an experience I wouldn't wish on anybody. And it was not the best use for alcohol. I swore abominably – it helped to a degree. But in between the curses, I did apologise to the lovely nurses whose job it was to hold me down. To tell the truth, perhaps not all the nurses were the beauties I now imagine them to have been. But during the two months of the Rising I was treated in a grand total of seven hospitals, where the nurses were such angels that even now they still wear the halo of my gratitude and remembrance.

My smart uniform and high boots had disappeared, lost irretrievably. I found myself in bed practically naked. One of the volunteer nurses recognised me – we had met once before at the house of some mutual friends. That chance encounter almost certainly saved my life.

The hospital was packed with wounded, most of them civilians. In the bed next to mine a young man was dying of tetanus, his body distorted by terrible spasms. He must have suffered agonies. His cries were difficult to bear, even though I was semiconscious, in a kind of fog, my head humming like an engine. Next morning my nurse-acquaintance suddenly materialised by my bed, accompanied by another girl. Carrying me on a stretcher they ran into the street. My head seemed to clear a little. 'What's happening?' I asked. 'The Krauts are coming,' said my would-be friend. 'They are sure to finish off the wounded.'

They got me out just in time. The streets were full of rubble. Every few hundred yards they were blocked by uprooted trees, pavement stones, pieces of furniture, thrown on top of one another helter-skelter by civilians attempting to make barricades. But though they obstructed our progress, they weren't nearly sturdy enough to stop, or even delay, the tanks. To this day, I don't understand how those two girls, both slight and both under twenty, managed to carry an adult man weighing some sixty kilograms two or three kilometres from one hospital to another, while the barricaded streets were one long obstacle course.

The Hospital of the Knights of Malta was a real hospital run by nuns, properly trained nurses, helped by the young women volunteers of the Underground. To the best of my recollection I stayed there for about four days from 6 August. As soon as I realised that Grzybowska Street, where I rented a flat in the name of Wichowski, was not far from the hospital, I asked a stranger, a lady who happened to be there, to bring me some clothes: a pair of trousers, a shirt, a pair of shoes. She promised to do it and left, but she never came back. Maybe she didn't go. Perhaps she was killed. In any case, I did not get my clothes.

After three days I started to hobble, my right leg still far from good. But I wanted to leave the hospital, the sooner the better. I feared that the Germans were only too likely to take it. I was right, though I didn't learn the whole story until very much later. The Germans did take the hospital, but for a change they didn't murder the patients. Twenty of the latter were wounded German prisoners and as the Polish staff had treated them on a par with us, their testimony worked a miracle: the entire hospital staff and the wounded were given safe passage to the city centre, which was in Polish hands.

I left before that happened, but in order to do so I needed some clothing. All I had on me was an unashamedly short shirt and a hospital blanket. Using the blanket as a kind of cloak, I went in search of help. The first nun I came across seemed like a good soul. 'Sister,' I pleaded with her, 'Would you find me a pair of trousers, a jacket and some shoes? Please . . .'

'I don't have any,' she cut me off curtly. But my mind was made up. God forgive me, but I couldn't think of any other way. I spread my arms wide, thus giving the nun a full frontal view of my near-nakedness. 'What are you doing?' she cried out loud, covering her eyes. But within five minutes I was dressed, perhaps not smartly, but completely, from top to bottom. I crossed the hospital garden, found a hole in the wall and was on my way to the Old Town.

On the corner of Długa and Kiliński Streets a big office block had been converted into another makeshift hospital. With great difficulty I hobbled into it. Suddenly, I was surrounded by a crowd of enthusiastic, under-employed nurses; as yet they'd had only a few casualties. The gaggle of girls included Halinka, a pretty girl of seventeen whom I had known in the old days in Konstancin. Within minutes all my wounds were re-dressed by several girls competing for the privilege. They were beginners and their ministrations were rather amateurish, but I was a willing victim. In the evening they even put on a kind of a theatrical performance for patients.

But this was the calm between two storms.

SEVENTEEN

The Warsaw Rising 2
(11 August 1944)

THE TELEPHONES WERE STILL WORKING and I was able to make enquiries. I learned about Olek's death in Żolibórz. Stefan Graf, my workmate from Pfeiffer's, had also been killed. The attempt by my unit to take the German police barracks in Wola, the attack in which I had been wounded, had failed. Even worse, it was followed by a massive wide-fronted German onslaught on Wola, making the insurgents fall back towards the Old Town. The aim of this German offensive from the west was to reinforce their positions along the strategically important east–west route. The inhabitants of Wola, who had greeted us with open arms in the first days of the Rising, were mercilessly slaughtered by the SS. Practically the entire population of the quarter, somewhere between 80,000 and 100,000 people, mainly women, children and old people, were driven from their homes and murdered.

In their retreat, my friends spent the night in the Pfeiffer tannery. To proceed further they had to reclaim Stawki, the quarter originally taken by us and by now retaken by the Germans. It was not an easy task, as the road was barred by a tank and they had no anti-tank weapons. In this second attack on Stawki, Janusz and Janek were killed at the same time; in all our previous battles my place was always next to them. Olszyna, an assistant professor of Warsaw University and second-in-command to Józef Rybicki, the OC of the Warsaw *Kedyw*, also fell. Zygmunt, a friend from the vocational school, was another casualty. It was soon after he had heard of the death of his fiancée, Zosia; quite possibly he had lost his will to live. In this one day I learned of the deaths of eleven close friends.

My wounds were still troublesome, but I was reasonably mobile and I set out to look for my unit. The first detachment I came across was made up of boys from Wola, most of them industrial workers. They were in trouble, having been accused of disobedience. The problem was that our unit had lost several officers in quick succession and command had passed to Śnica. He was older than most of us and had completed his officer training before the war. There was no denying his personal bravery but, unfortunately, he lacked common sense and any ability to foresee the consequences of his actions. He had a perfect right to risk his own life, but he gave little thought to the lives of his subordinates, setting them impossible tasks. When he ordered a frontal attack on the tank barring the road, the boys had refused to follow his order. Śnica reported them for 'insubordination in the face of the enemy'. It *was* insubordination, there could be no doubt about it, but the attack would have been suicidal. I found those boys disarmed and sulking, but eventually managed to talk them into rejoining the unit. Subsequently, they fought with great courage and determination throughout the Rising, in spite of heavy casualties.

Two or three days after my arrival in the Old Town, I suddenly heard shouts of joy and cries of 'hurrah!' just outside the hospital. I went to the window. On the corner of the street, a small tank captured from the Germans was surrounded by an enthusiastic crowd. I was still very slow on my feet and hadn't yet managed to get downstairs when a huge blast shook the building. Plaster came down from the ceiling and the whole building trembled as if shaken by an earthquake. I hobbled back to the window. The tank had disappeared, and in its place there was a large crater in the road. The vehicle had been a trap, a Trojan horse. Filled with explosives and fitted with a detonator, it was a time bomb.

No less than 200 people were killed and the number of wounded was even greater. The area was littered with bodies. Those standing near the tank had been thrown into the upper floors of nearby houses. From every direction there came the cries of the wounded. From being a patient, I turned into a nurse. Now I was looking for the husband of one wounded woman, now for the child of another . . . Within minutes, the near-empty hospital filled with casualties. I needed a moment's rest and found a place in the cellar next to a man with severe burns. He had been one of the firefighters when an incendiary bomb hit the ground next to him. He was groaning with pain, while his wife and children sat with him, crying. I couldn't bear it any longer and left the cellar as fast as I could. There were now no more vacant beds in this hospital, and besides I'd had enough. I was about to leave the building when I came across one of our boys, Remec, from the Mokotów unit of *Kedyw*. He told me that the remnant of my troop were defending the John of God Church and mental hospital. Soon the two of us were on our way to rejoin them in action. I could just about walk, with difficulty.

The relentless, heavy German fire continued. Artillery shells, rockets and other assorted missiles were falling all around us. Particularly unpleasant were the heavy shells known to us as 'cows' or 'wardrobes' because their explosion was preceded by a noise like cattle lowing, or a heavy wardrobe being pushed about. Having reached the Old Town we stopped for a short rest. This saved us from a 'cow' which exploded a few metres ahead. We reached the John of God Church just in time to bury one of our boys, killed by a bullet which had cut the artery in his neck.

We held the position for several days. The hospital doors now stood open and, lost in a crazy world of their own, some of the unattended mental patients kept strolling backwards and forwards in the no man's land. Inevitably, some were hit. Some found shelter in the cellars of the Old Town, adding to the chaos that had overtaken the civilian population.

A very bleak picture of these days has remained with me until now; I still see the crazed patients strolling under fire in the no man's land, falling, trails of their blood making patterns on the ground.

Another memory is of a seemingly ghostly apparition. One day, as we were defending Konwiktorska Street, I went to investigate a strange noise coming from the outside. The *Polonia* football ground across the street was in German hands. The noise came from a figure clad in nothing but a long shirt, shuffling across to our position. This was happening in plain view of the enemy, who were not known for sparing anybody, but somehow they held their fire. The strange man entered, holding an empty jar in his hands. Politely, he kept offering us pickled cucumbers and honey for sale. For once I was lost for words. 'The quartermaster is in the back,' I told him eventually. He went to look for him with his 'wares'.

Under unrelenting German pressure, we had to abandon the church and took up our position in apartment blocks at the far end of the hospital garden. Our leaders, however, decided the church had to be retaken, as it was strategically important for the defence of the Old Town. Columbus, at the head of ten lads, was to mount an attack across the hospital garden while I, with seven men, was to proceed through the cellars and attack simultaneously on the right flank. We climbed out of a basement window and ran towards the church. It was nine or ten in the evening and quite dark, but the Germans must have heard us. As I learned later, Columbus was wounded in the knee right at the beginning and his attack lost its momentum. My group found shelter behind a brick wall about twenty centimetres high. The Germans turned a flame-thrower on us, but luckily we were not within its range. Though it did not do us any harm, it did stop us from gaining more ground. I found a piece of an old plank. 'Touch wood,' I said. 'Now we'll be safe.' Somebody laughed. And so I discovered that in a tight spot a cool head and a bit of humour may save the situation, perhaps even lives . . .

I decided to fall back to our starting position. In the cellar I counted heads. One boy was missing. We were about to look for him outside when he returned unaided, though with a serious head wound. Taken to the Crooked Lantern makeshift hospital, he was later murdered in its cellars, as were most of the other patients.

My wounds from the days in Wola were still oozing. A friend of mine, Zbylut, a fifth year medical student, dressed and redressed them, but proud flesh prevented proper scar formation. One of the Salonikan Greek Jews whom we liberated in Stawki was a doctor, an old man of at least forty-five or fifty. Zbylut asked him to have a look at my injuries. Their only common language was Latin. It was the oddest consultation. In spite of its loftiness, even in November 1944 my wounds were still giving me trouble.

We defended the Old Town for twenty days. The day-by-day details can easily be found in reference books. It suffices to say that we endured those twenty days under constant artillery fire from Praga across the river, amidst exploding rockets and 'cows' and under repeated aerial bombardment. The Germans used only four bombers. They would come over, drop their load of incendiary bombs – both half-ton and small – on us, turn back to reload and deface the cloudless Warsaw sky with another bombing mission forty minutes later. They had the sky to themselves; the Red Army was stationed just across the Vistula, but not a single Soviet fighter challenged them. Bombing Warsaw was as easy as a turkey shoot, and just as safe for the crews.

The civilian population survived in the cellars as best they could. The intervening walls had been demolished in places to allow free passage between individual cellars, and the latter-day cavemen could circulate underground without having to venture into the streets. We used the upper floors for sleeping in. Flats were empty and offered a choice of bedrooms, even of libraries if one was so inclined. They were infinitely more congenial than the cellars. More dangerous? Yes, but some of us had become practising fatalists.

One day, four lads were playing bridge while off duty. Somebody discovered a gramophone and some records; so we had music to relax by. Stretched out on a sofa, I was reading a book. Suddenly, a deafening explosion interrupted my reverie. The ceiling plaster came down and a cloud of dust filled the room. Stoically the bridge players swept the rubble off the table and continued their game. But not for long. A three-storey wing of the house, on the other side of the central courtyard, was brought down suddenly by a 'cow'. We had to rescue people buried under the rubble. End of our rest.

Another day, I was inspecting the lookouts placed in the garrets of the buildings in our front line. One of the lads was standing clearly silhouetted against the clear, blue evening sky, even at a distance. The dry weather continued and fires burned unchallenged by a single drop of rain. I lost my temper. 'You fool!' I shouted. 'Do you want to cop it? The Krauts can see you plain as day.'

'See for yourself,' replied the boy. 'Can I lie down here?' And indeed, a rafter of the ruined house was alive, covered with a column of bedbugs on the move. Thousands of them marching, a second bloodthirsty enemy army, though this one only on parade. I ordered him to a new observation post.

Soon after, there was a memorable death. The boy must have joined up late, after the Rising had started. I didn't know him well and I have forgotten both his name and his pseudonym. He was hit at his lookout post on the fourth floor. We carried him downstairs to bury him in the yard. Amazingly, we found a ready-made grave. Somebody must have dug it just in case. I didn't give it much thought. There was a constant demand. We buried our friend's body. Somebody said a prayer. We stood over the grave at attention for a minute's silence.

We had just started on the way back to our quarters when I heard a scream: 'Bloody hell! They've stolen our grave!' A group of soldiers was coming from the other side of the courtyard, bearing another body. They didn't seem pleased – quite the opposite. We had to clear out in a hurry.

But this tragi-comical episode was an exception. The general atmosphere was far from jovial. The conditions were dreadful, especially for the civilian population, camped in the cellars: women, old people and children, the escaped mental patients roaming amongst them. At first, the civilians accepted the situation with a mixture of enthusiasm and resignation. But soon their forbearance began to wear thin. Towards the end of August we were met with hostility and often with rage, while using the underground passages.

On the day of the bridge party, on 25 August to be precise, the news spread – probably from the radio-monitoring service of the Home Army – that Paris had been liberated. It filled me with unmitigated envy. I happened to be talking to Jodła as we heard the news. I had known him well as Roman's schoolmate in Garwolin and subsequently as our tenant for several months in Żolibórz. Unbeknownst to me he had found his way into *Kedyw*, and I met him again at the start of the Rising. I clearly remember saying to him 'Perhaps the Krauts will capitulate now that they have lost Paris. If not, we are finished. There they got rid of them in three days, while we shall all perish here before Warsaw is free . . .'

At the time we knew nothing, of course, of either the help given to the Paris insurgents or of General de Gaulle's negotiations with the Americans, which facilitated General Leclerc's division to save the French capital.

Under constant German pressure, the part of the Old Town we held kept shrinking. On 26 or 27 August we lost the State Mint, a big concrete building and thus an important northern bulwark of the Old Town's defence. We were posted to Zakroczymska Street to fill the gap in our lines. By then our strength was down from the original seventy five men to about twenty, and that included several walking wounded like myself, the rest having been either killed or hospitalised.

About that time an old friend, Antoni, unexpectedly rejoined us. He had lost part of his hand in June, before the Rising, in our somewhat unorthodox attack on the Gestapo car in Żolibórz. Having learnt that we were in the Old Town, he pleaded to be posted to us. As the Old Town was surrounded, this was a difficult proposition. He made his way through the city sewers, partly on his knees, carrying his rifle above his head, and reached us just as we were at the end of our tether.

Our next task was to take the houses along Kościelna Street. Antoni with eight lads was to attack from the corner of Franciszkańska Street, and I, with the remaining seven, from Zakroczymska Street. To do so we had to pass to the right of an old palace which, at the time of the 1830 rising against the Russians, became the barracks of Czwartacy, a famous regiment of infantry.

We advanced. There was no sign of Antoni's force. I sent a lad to reconnoitre. He came back with the news that Antoni's detachment had been eliminated by a single howitzer shell which left them all wounded, Antoni in both legs. They had been taken to the Crooked Lantern hospital. And so, left on our own, our strength reduced to eight, we tried to take the shell of a burnt-out building across the street. Incredibly, it was still standing, though its walls had been weakened by fire. A German soldier tried to stop us with a flame-thrower. A sudden blast of wind turned the flames back onto him. I must admit that all I felt was relief.

We were inside the burnt-out house when we heard the aeroplanes and explosions. They usually came in two or three waves. The next lot of bombs, or the one after, was bound to be for us. I ordered a retreat across the street, where a carriage gateway offered a more solid-looking cover than the barely upright walls of the burnt-out house – or so I thought. I counted my men. One was missing. I was not going to retreat with my detachment incomplete so I stayed behind with Zbylut, our doctor, who kept me company out of sheer friendship. 'Broda, Broda!' we kept calling the missing lad, when the bombs came down. Blasts . . . deafening noise . . . falling bricks, black dust . . . flying chunks of plaster . . . When the dust settled, my boys were nowhere to be seen. The 'safe' gateway across the street took a direct hit. They were all buried. In the middle of the road, about five or ten metres from us, lay a half-ton unexploded bomb. Zbylut and I owed our lives to a saboteur slave-labourer in a German munitions factory – maybe a Pole.

I could see the head of one of my boys protruding from the rubble of the gateway. This seventeen-year-old volunteer had joined us only two or three days before. He kept crying out with pain. I ran to him. '*Panie poruczniku*, Lieutenant Sir, I am sorry, please forgive my screaming.' We started digging him out, but we couldn't manage on our own. I ran into the nearby Franciscan Church. The crypt was crowded. 'My boys are buried, I need help!' Nobody stirred, not a soul. An obviously fit man in his prime stood next to me. I turned to him: 'You are coming with me!'

'Not me,' he answered, and didn't budge.

Furious, I stuck my *Parabellum* in his belly. 'Move, or I'll shoot.' This time he responded.

We managed to dig the boy out. Both his legs were fractured. I sent him to the Crooked Lantern hospital. Along with others, he was murdered there by German troops a couple of days later.

All my other soldiers were buried deep under the rubble. Among the dead was Budrys, whom we had entrusted with a leather bag containing the chronicle of our unit from the first day of the Rising. I was certain that the document was irretrievably lost, but it surfaced again in 1989. The bag and its contents had been found during the clearance of the ruins of the Old Town soon after the war, and the damaged loose leaves, difficult to decipher, were entrusted to Józef Rybicki. Under the Stalinist regime in Poland, the secret police raided and searched his flat again and again. If found, this valuable document would have been confiscated and the eye-witness evidence had to be protected. In fact, Rybicki had hidden it so well that in later years he himself lost sight of it. Much later, after his death, his daughter Hanna discovered the cache, deciphered and copied the notes and passed them on to Mr Giedroyć, in Maison Lafitte near Paris.

Mr Giedroyć has been publishing *Kultura*, a Polish political review, since 1946, having started it in cooperation with Mr Czapski, a well-known writer. Our diary appeared in print in *Zeszyty Historyczne*, or *Historical Notes*, an offshoot of *Kultura* issue No. 94.

EIGHTEEN

The Warsaw Rising 3
(29 August 1944)

I MAY BE SOMEWHAT INACCURATE IN MY CHRONOLOGY, but as far as I remember the events described below happened on or around 29 August 1944.

Zbylut and I rejoined the rest of our unit defending the Kościelna Street church. Śnica and Kryst, both sharp-shooters, took up position in the attic of an adjoining building. They had a good view of the gardens of the Czwartacy barracks, and put quite a few Krauts out of action. Two German soldiers tried to hide by using the back of a sofa as a shield. Two almost simultaneous gunshots and both soldiers were flat on the ground with the settee as their ready-made coffin.

At 10 p.m. on 30 August, I received the order to withdraw my men from their positions and pull back to 7 Kozla Street, our main quarters. The movement was to be executed silently, so as not to attract the enemy's attention. This order startled me; who the hell was going to replace us? I took it up with the segment commander. 'Just carry out the order,' he said. Then I understood: we were abandoning the Old Town – after thirty days of stubborn and costly resistance. And what route were we going to use? The shattered streets or the subterranean sewers?

Eventually, the former route was chosen. On 31 August we reached our starting position: the Bank Polski building on Bielańska Street. To get there we had to push through a dense crowd of people waiting for a break-out. Who could have ordered this concentration?

I was called to a briefing by Major Trzaska in the presence of Major Jan. The Old Town had been reduced to rubble and further defence of it had become impossible. To open the way out, a company of the

Zośka battalion, commanded by Andrzej Morro, was to attack from the bank building and across the rubble towards Bank Square. We were to follow. The objective was to open the way from the Old Town to the capital's centre. Once a passage had been opened through the ring of German forces, other units were to follow in a stipulated order, the medics collecting the wounded on the way. Major Jan was to stay with us. Wigry, the assault company, was to attack on our left flank along Senatorska Street, between the bank and Teatralny Square. The attack was set for midnight. The evacuation of the Old Town was to be completed between 2 and 3 a.m.

We, the remainder of *Kedyw*, all twenty of us, were waiting in front of the bank among the rubble. Though the attack was to have begun at midnight, it was now 1 a.m. and nothing was happening. It was nearly 3 a.m. by the time the order reached us. Much too late.

Morro's group was the first to run across the street. Then it was our turn. 'Let's go,' ordered Major Jan. The ground was strewn with rubble, but there was a wall still standing on our left. The German fire, tracing bullets, didn't ease off even for a moment and covered the ground with mounds of plaster, coming off the wall.

'Let's proceed on the left, under cover of the wall,' I suggested to Śnica.

'No way,' he snapped back. 'The order is to attack straight ahead, on the right.' There was no time to argue. Śnica was like that. He was willing to die himself and take us all with him. Not an ounce of common sense.

Luckily, Major Jan arrived. 'Let's move on the left along the wall,' he ordered. The obvious route. He ran a little in advance and to the left of the rest of us, along Senatorska Street. The Wigry company ought to have been there, but there was no sign of them. Suddenly we heard a cry of '*Hände hoch*!' and Jan fell, mown down by German fire.

We ran under cover of the wall, in a kind of canyon between it and mounds of rubble. I slowed down. Two weeks in hospital and unhealed wounds were telling. I straggled in the tail, yet I hated my weakness to show. I tried again and again to keep up. I couldn't. Suddenly, a two-metre-high wall blocked our way. The boys went over the top. It was beyond my strength. Somebody helped me over.

We joined what was left of Morro's company in another burnt-out house across the street from St Anthony's church. Continuous heavy machine-gun fire made the street impassable. On our side we were partly protected by the wall.

The sky was getting lighter. It was dawn.

None of the other units had followed us, and the German ring closed in behind. We were surrounded. The attempt to break out of the Old Town had failed.

We took up position in one wing of a block of flats. The Germans, confident of their superiority, ran forward and were met with grenades. There were sixty of us, surrounded by Germans. Saski Park was in front of us, the building of the Bank Polski behind. Retreat was impossible. No medics had followed us to carry out the wounded scattered along our path; they all perished, finished off by the enemy. But it didn't matter any more. We were all destined to die. Here or there, what difference did it make?

We heard Morro calling us from the church, but machinegun fire made his words incomprehensible. He leapt forward followed by Witold, and they dashed across the street. They reached us, both lightly wounded.

An impasse. Then Morro gave an order and two impact grenades were thrown into the street. A huge explosion . . . a cloud of dust – almost a smoke screen. The machinegun fire stopped. We raced across the street and into the church, losing one man at the start. Morro got a bullet through the fleshy part of his nose but did not fall back.

We were inside the church, on our own, cut off from the rest of the town. There was no chance of any support or rescue. All entrances had to be covered. With Zbylut, my doctor friend, we took position in a small yard adjoining the church, next to one of the church doors. Zbylut sat down with his back to the wall, just under a slit in the wall roughly cut by somebody to use as an embrasure. I sat in a niche of the same wall, several metres to his right. We felt secure, out of the enemy's sight.

Suddenly, a gunshot. Zbylut fell forward. He was crawling towards me on all fours when I saw bullets hitting his head. I was about to send a round from my Thompson into the embrasure, but the weapon jammed; the dust of those three days of continuous bombardment must have got into it. Zbylut lay motionless at my feet. More shots. I felt something hitting my left side. The bullets had to be coming from the roof or the hole in the wall. They found their target in my left buttock. Only later did I realise that we had been in full view of the Ukrainian SS men on the upper floors of an adjacent house.

Within moments two nurses, Danka and her friend, ran to us with coffin carriers in place of stretchers and took us into the church. Zbylut was dying. Having placed me on my belly, the girls attended to my wound. A bullet had made a tunnel through my buttocks from left to right. To this day, the site of the wound is a source of much merriment.

'I won't be able to walk,' I thought. Disgusted with my jammed Thompson gun, I cleaned and readied my *Parabellum*. The Germans or Ukrainians were bound to finish us off any minute. I decided to blow my brains out, having first taken one or two of them with me. Better than being kicked to death – we heard the cries of one of our wounded being thus treated before we ran into the church.

Lying there face down on a coffin carrier among the church paraphernalia, I was convinced that I had at most an hour to live. Ought I pray? A Polish saying came to me: '*Jak trwoga to do Boga*', or 'In mortal peril one turns to God'. Didn't they say that there were no atheists in foxholes?

Amidst the horrors of war I had lost faith a few years back. And now, in a church, next to a dying comrade, facing my own death, I decided to remain true to myself. I would not pray. Was I making a mistake? Perhaps when we did meet, God would respect my decision and congratulate me on my determination to stick to my principles. That meeting has not taken place yet, so I don't know what His answer will be.

In the meantime, Morro and Trzaska had made their decision. At about 6 a.m. an order was passed from mouth to mouth, and in absolute silence we crossed the church garden into another burnt-out building in Albert King of the Belgians Street. I was lucky; mine was only a flesh wound, and I managed, with difficulty, to follow the others. As I learned later, our new abode was the old Zamoyski Palace. Palace or not, it was now just a shell, its walls still hot from the fire which had destroyed it and even now still smouldering here and there. It was warm outside, but here it felt like a hot furnace.

We waited and waited. What for? For how long? We hid in the corridor. I was resting on my belly, next to a lad lying on his side, nursing his arm wounds. We had to keep absolute silence, but how do you keep quiet a man with his arm in shreds?

Outside, the enemy kept patrolling the street. We saw their boots high up in the cellar windows. At first they had no idea where we had disappeared to, but at about 11 a.m. they must have heard some noise, and dropped several grenades into the cellars just in case. Explosions. Clouds of dust. Then silence. The dust and smoke were choking us. We had all taken cover in niches and behind bits of walls, still upright. There were no new casualties. Then came more explosions. A short series of machinegun fire hit the walls next to the windows. All was quiet again. Another impasse: the enemy was wary of charging the cellars. In the evening, the heat inside must have exceeded forty degrees centigrade. Rivulets of sweat ran into my eyes, my wounds hurt, the grenades dropped in regularly provided the only distraction. The scarce water was reserved for the wounded.

A whispered order reached me; we were to wait until darkness and then cross the enemy lines to join our forces on the other side of the Saski Park.

This must have been the longest day of my life.

At 9 p.m., after the last head count, we filed out very quietly through a small window into the garden. Night-flying moths would have seemed noisy compared with us. Suddenly, 'Down!' The order made us cling to the ground. Three German lorries packed with military police passed just a few paces from us. Then we were up again, marching in tight formation across the Saski Park in the direction of the Polish line. We wove our way between the enemy's positions and dug-outs. What saved us were the German camouflage jackets and helmets captured on the first day of the Rising which we wore now, with the Polish red-and-white armbands tucked away safely in our pockets.

Unchallenged, we reached Marszałkowska Street. We had to cross it. A road block barred our way. '*Halt! Wo is da*? Who goes there? Password!' In perfect German, Dobrosław from the Zośka battalion asked for directions 'to the positions of the Polish bandits'. We were a special detachment sent from headquarters, he said. 'Password!' repeated the guard. 'You, soldier,' Dobrosław got visibly angry, 'Attention! Coming from our own side? You idiot! What do you want a password for?'

The guard stood to attention, clicking his heels. '*Jawohl. Go,*' he opened the way. We ran into Królewska Street.

Jumping from one heap of rubble to another shook me to the core. The new wound hurt like hell. Running towards our lines we yelled at the top of our voices: 'Radosław! We are Poles! Don't shoot!' There was one shot. One of our boys fell dead. But then, fortunately, they believed us. There was no more firing. We were in the city centre.

I learned much later that Socha and two other young men had been left behind in the cellar. They were guarding the other end of the cellar and the whispered order failed to reach them. Having realised that they were left on their own they followed the same route, crawling for part of it, and all three reached the Polish line.

We couldn't have had a more enthusiastic reception. I badly needed to get to a hospital, but first I had to join the others in hymn singing. Yet, exhausted after three days of fighting with practically no sleep, I wasn't up to celebrations and as soon as I decently could, I reported wounded. The field hospital had been set up in the cellars of the PKO (Polish Savings Bank) building. The nurses there greeted me as an old friend. It was the relocated Knights of Malta Hospital, in which I had found refuge with my first wounds in early August. The girls washed me, fed me, made a detailed list of my old and new wounds and lacerations, dressed them, and practically kissed me good-night; but even so, after three sleepless nights I was too exhausted to sleep.

On 1 September, a surgeon decided to operate on me. 'Minor surgery,' he pronounced. He cut the skin and muscles of my left buttock, so as to lay open the tunnel the bullet had made through it. For some reason he didn't do the same on the right side and for over a year afterwards I could sit on only one half of that part of my anatomy which is designed to work as a whole. Eventually, an abscess developed and burst. The discharge contained a piece of my trousers which had been carried deep into the wound by the bullet.

Two or three days after this minor surgery, I was able to move about and started looking for my friends. I found the remnants of our detachment having a few days' rest in the city centre, where most houses were still, miraculously, intact. Even the windows retained their windowpanes. One could not compare it to the Old Town, an area of burnt-out shells. One day a local detachment of the Home Army invited three of us to dinner in an underground hall. They wanted to know more about our exploits in August. No sooner did we start eating than an alarm was sounded. We did not use alarm sirens in the Old Town; they would never have ceased. Here, in a twinkle of an eye the hall emptied and only the three of us, veterans, were left alone. We just put our steel helmets on and continued with the meal. Our hosts, having disappeared to a lower level, re-emerged, shamefaced, some time later to rejoin us.

Let me return for a while to the fate of my friends left behind in the Old Town. Once the gap which we had made in the tight German ring at street level was closed and the enemy line reformed, the surrounded Polish fighters had no alternative but to make their way out through the sewers. All the survivors, the unscathed and the walking wounded alike, had to descend into the stinking subterranean guts of the city. Luckily, I had been spared this loathsome experience. My old friends, among them Stasinek, blinded and led by his wife, Columbus, who was wounded in the leg, and our doctor Jerzy, managed to reach the city centre. Jerzy described their trek in some detail. They walked up to their waists in the stinking mess. In places the passage was too low to walk upright, and they had to proceed on their knees as if they were on some pilgrimage to hell. Wounded and exhausted men and women would fall and drown. In a few hopeless cases, the medics spared their suffering with lethal injections of morphine. It was a nightmarish journey, but it saved many lives. The Germans were not in the habit of taking prisoners; all insurgents were shot, even the wounded, wherever they were found. The civilian population of the Old Town was allowed out, but had to leave all their possessions behind.

I was told by Remec in 1945 about the fate of the seriously wounded left in the cellars of the Crooked Lantern hospital. He himself, with about fifteen others, had asked to be taken out of the cellars and they were left lying in the street. When the Germans arrived they shot all the wounded in the building. This murderous task accomplished, they transferred their attention to those in the street. On seeing them approach, Remec stretched out his arm in the direction of their commanding officer and made the sign of the cross.

'What are you doing?' asked the German.

'I am a priest,' replied Remec. 'Just before you shoot us, I wish to forgive you and bless you while I can . . .' This spark of genius saved the entire group. Even the Nazi officer was bowled over by the magnanimity of the Polish clergyman. In fact Remec, a handsome ladies' man, could not have been further from a priestly vocation.

The entire group was then taken to the Wola hospital. Remec could not yet abandon his role of priest, as patients kept asking him for prayers. But he, who hadn't said the Lord's Prayer for years, had forgotten one passage: 'Forgive us our trespasses as we forgive those who trespass against us.' The truncated paternoster was greeted with an ovation; how right the priest was, in the circumstances, to deny forgiveness to the Nazis.

The nuns who ran the hospital found a separate room for the 'priest'. And naturally other clergymen patients gathered around him, wanting to know which parish he came from, what seminary he had attended. Eventually Remec had to own up to his deception and to relate the entire, truly miraculous story. The nuns were not amused. He was returned to the general ward. To impersonate a priest was sacrilege, even if the deception saved fifteen lives. Some things are simply not done.

Several days after my arrival in the hospital, I learned that Stasinek, Columbus and several others were in another makeshift hospital in Marszałkowska Street, the other side of Jerozolimskie Avenue, an important east-west roadway which remained under constant German fire. There was a communication trench, but because of a railway tunnel under the street the trench could not be more than fifty to seventy centimetres deep. The things one does for one's friends . . .

Whereas in the Old Town the food reserves, particularly of sugar, captured in the Stawki stores were not too bad, the city centre was practically starving. One day somebody borrowed my *Parabellum* and went hunting. A basset hound had apparently been seen in the area. Another day somebody brought a dead chicken, a war casualty. But, unmistakably, it had been dead for some time. Cooked and re-cooked many times over, it was eventually eaten, but my participation was only of the olfactory kind.

Roman came to see me in hospital. He had asked Józef Rybicki whether he knew what happened to me. The other had no idea. 'Staś Likiernik?' he repeated, 'Who is he?'

'You do know him, you yourself christened him Maccabaeus.'

'Now you're talking,' said Rybicki on hearing my nickname; it wasn't until after the war that I learned who had been its originator. 'You'll find him in Marszałkowska Street.' Thinking that my fighting days were over, I gave Roman my *Parabellum*. Only for safe-keeping, I thought to myself as I crossed my fingers.

Soon after, somebody told us that fifteen of the *Kedyw* boys still capable of fighting had joined forces with the Zośka battalion and made their way to Czerniaków, a riverside quarter of the city. 'You ought to join them,' said our visitor. 'There are gardens there, allotments, plenty of fruit, vegetables. Vitamins, you know. Your wounds would have a chance to heal. Tomatoes . . .' he added, as if in a trance. As Stasinek was blind and Columbus had a nasty knee wound – his hobbling was worse than mine – I was delegated to explore the route. After much consultation and with the itinerary marked on my map, I limped out of the hospital. The tunnels in my buttocks, plus my old wounds in the back and the leg, slowed me down; at times very much so. If one followed Książęca Street, Czerniaków was not that far, only two kilometres, but it seemed to be moving further and further away. Eventually, I reached the corner of Rozbrat and Szara Streets. The gardens opposite, stretching up the slope of the Vistula valley towards the Sejm (Parliament) building, were in German hands.

In Czerniaków I was received with surprise. People talked all at once. 'Why the hell have you come here? The German attack on Czerniaków is imminent.' 'You should have stayed in the centre, you fool!'

On 7 September, the day of my arrival in Czerniaków, the Książęca Street route from the centre to the river was cut off by the enemy. After Wola and the Old Town, it was now the turn of Czerniaków to become the heart of the Rising.

NINETEEN

The Warsaw Rising 4
(Czerniaków)

I SPENT THE FIRST DAY IN CZERNIAKÓW RESTING, lodging in a house just two or three hundred metres from the front line. A priest, wearing a camouflage jacket like my own, came over to see me; we engaged in a long conversation. We had never met before, but I had heard of him. He was Father Paweł, the priest who had remained with Zośka, our friendly battalion, throughout the Rising. Much later I saw his picture in a book about the Old City and learned that his real name was Father Józef Warszawski.

He had time to spare that day. And so had I. For at least two hours we dealt with such timeless topics as God, faith and Jesus Christ. He was eloquent and convincing on the subject of Jesus and His love for us. But I was a doubting Thomas. I knew that faith was a blessing, but evidently I had not been so blessed. The episode a few days ago in St Anthony's church had only confirmed my lack of belief. So, to conclude the discussion, I asked a question: 'The Uprising is finished, Father, it's over, is it not?'

'Yes, it is.'

'Well then, shouldn't we surrender?'

'No, my son.'

'In this case, I shall follow your argument to its logical conclusion and not surrender either. I shall remain an agnostic. I have lost my faith. There is no return.'

'Think again, my son. Should your conscience stir, come tomorrow to take Holy Communion . . . I'll consider our conversation to be your confession . . .'

I thought and thought again. But I did not take up his offer.

The next minute, the German planes returned bearing their deadly cargo. Diving, dropping their bombs, which mercifully fell two hundred metres in front and two hundred metres behind our house, their silhouettes criss-crossing our glassless windows.

Next day Śnica came to see me. 'Janek Bagiński has been wounded. Will you replace him and take over the defence of half the building at the corner of Rozbrat and Szara Streets?' And so I returned to the front line, without my *Parabellum*, but armed with another revolver in my belt. I was just able to move about. I did not actually take part in the fighting. Instead I made a round of our position, effected a few changes here and there, and surveyed the enemy line.

A tank opened fire and the Germans attacked under its cover. As they entered Szara Street at a trot, Kryst, posted on the first-floor balcony, greeted them with grenades. Several men fell and the rest retreated. A body remained lying in the middle of the street. At great risk and against my explicit orders, one of our girls, Irys, crawled out of the cellar window to get his rifle and ammunition. She was in luck.

Soon after that repelled attack I happened to be outside in the courtyard of the block of flats when a howitzer shell landed, creating havoc: one of our boys was killed outright, a girl lost her leg; I was sprayed with shrapnel from top to bottom. One of them hit my right arm.

Strangely, this shell saved my life.

I had had enough of hospitals in cellars, of people dying around me, of lost hopes, of needless suffering. And here I was wounded again. I'd really had enough. We were all going to die anyway – I might as well end it all now. A bullet in my temple and I would know no more. My revolver was still in my belt, I could feel its weight on my belly; I reached out, but couldn't make it. My right arm was useless, paralysed – that damn shell – I tried to reach the gun with my left arm . . . I couldn't. It's jolly awkward to reach with your left hand a gun stuck in your belt. Just then the two girls, Zosia and Danka, knelt by my side, held my arm and started removing the splinters of metal, most of them embedded just skin deep. One, very close to my right eye, I removed myself. But they were everywhere. Even in the most intimate parts of my anatomy. However, I did manage to produce children when the time came. Now, aeons later, Zosia and Danka still smile knowingly at the memory of my wounds.

I was not able to get up, so the girls decided to carry me to the Okrąg Street hospital. They had to run four or five hundred metres carrying my dead weight. A German sniper tried to get us from a house top. 'Leave me here!' I screamed at the girls. 'Or all three of us will be dead. Take cover!' But they didn't obey. Polish women are like that: obstinate, disobedient, opinionated. All through the Rising our girls were incredibly brave. In the Old City I had seen a girl of seventeen or eighteen drag, all alone and under a shower of bullets, a big, heavy wounded man out of harm's way. But we were in luck. It must have been the sniper's bad day, and we reached our destination unscathed, or rather without any new injuries. I found myself in a cellar, next to another wounded man. I was not allowed food, not even water, as apparently one of the splinters was lodged in my belly. At some stage I must have passed out. I came round to find one of the volunteer nurses taking off my trousers. 'You naughty, filthy man,' she muttered. I must have soiled myself while I was unconscious. It really wasn't my fault . . .

Once again, as before in the Knights of Malta Hospital, I lay there clad only in my shirt. Anyway, I couldn't walk. My left leg, like a well prepared leg of mutton, was 'larded', though with metal fragments.

Suddenly, I heard shouts – in German! And very close to us! They were about to attack again, and soon. 'Help me out!' I called to one of our retreating soldiers, a young lad. He nodded. With my left arm round his neck – my right one was still useless – he dragged me across the passage to another cellar, further away from the entrance. This was occupied by two ladies nursing their wounded husbands, feeding them stewed apples. We heard the Germans shouting, closing in. 'Stewed apples?' I thought, 'We are in a stew already – why not?' and extended my working arm. Words were not necessary. They did not know about the nil-by-mouth doctor's orders and handed me a cupful.

In the meantime, a 'Goliath', a miniature electrically guided tank filled with explosives, reached the cellar which I had just vacated and blew up; my wounded neighbour was given no chance. Was he the lucky one? At that moment, and entirely by chance, my very old friend Irka, a qualified nurse (and later a doctor) noticed me, after a moment's hesitation recognised me, and decided to move me to another makeshift hospital in a Wilanowska Street cellar. She summoned help, and with a chair for a stretcher, I was carried to the new location.

Once more I found myself in a small cellar, under the care of my doctor, Jerzy, and a very pretty nurse. It must have been 13 or 14 September. Jerzy diagnosed peritonitis and ordered nil-by-mouth again. I was still naked except for my shirt, a rather short one at that, though, strangely, I had been allowed to keep my heavy marching boots. God knows why, as walking was out of the question; but they too played a part in the story.

History noted two important events about this particular time: firstly, the Soviet Army, including Polish units (commanded by General Berling), reached the Vistula and occupied its east bank opposite our positions: secondly, several *Kukuruzniks*, small planes with engines which sounded like motorcycles, dropped food and some weapons for us, but without parachutes these badly needed supplies mostly reached us damaged. Some of General Berling's Polish units crossed to our side of the river. Several men, speaking with the characteristic accents of eastern Poland, passed through our cellar. However, they had crossed the river at dawn, almost in daylight, instead of under the cover of darkness. General Berling had been waiting for the order of his Soviet commander, an order which never came. And so, having wasted most of the night, the Polish general gave the belated order himself. These units, moreover, had no training in close urban combat and sustained enormous losses.

Even this kind of help, however weak and futile, coming when all was lost, still went against the policy of Stalin, that of letting the Germans annihilate the best of the Polish nation.

But let's leave history to the historians. I do not recall the exact date when our able-bodied comrades had to leave us to the mercies of the approaching enemy; and we knew only too well what that meant. It was an awful moment. By now, apart from me there were two other casualties in the cellar, attended by Irka and the other nurse. In addition there were several other people walking in and out, including a lady doctor whom, immobilised in my corner of the cellar, I did not meet. 'The Krauts have nasty habits,' I warned all and sundry. 'If you don't want to be shot outright, get rid of every bit of German issue uniform, or anything which even remotely resembles it.'

There was a tiny glimmer of hope. Hitherto, as armed civilians, we were liable to be shot on sight, but on 1 September our western allies announced that we, the Polish Home Army, were *combatants* and must be treated in accordance with the Geneva Convention. This declaration had been inexplicably long in coming, but better late than never. Anyhow, this new exalted status proved illusory, at least in Czerniaków.

After the departure of our soldiers, we were alone and all was reasonably quiet for several hours. Suddenly, the peace was broken by ear-splitting shouts: '*Raus*, all those capable out . . . out . . .

upstairs,' accompanied by the loud clatter of steel heel-caps, rifle shots and screams of the wounded being murdered next door.

A German soldier appeared in the door of our cellar. He noticed Irka and the other nurse who – against orders – both stayed with us, and still blocking the door with his ample figure he motioned to the girls to stay put and his short '*Shön fertig*, all done,' stopped the others from bursting in. It was only after the war that Irka told me she had discovered his surname: it was *Freitag*, Man Friday.

Time passed. One hour, perhaps two. Then another German rushed into our cellar, a big fellow, a *Feldwebel*. He stood there in the semidarkness and after a while he noticed me. He was slow on the uptake. He sized me up. Wounded, still breathing, eyes open. This must be a mistake! Then his eyes rested on my marching boots. He grabbed my leg. '*Deutsche Schuhe!*' he screamed, drew his gun and aimed it at my head. But before he pulled the trigger, he noticed another casualty hiding in the darkness. His attention was distracted: '*Zweite Bandit*, another bandit!' he shouted.

Fortunately for me, our *Feldwebel* was not methodical enough to finish one job before starting another. The third occupant of our cellar, a much older man, spoke fluent German and said 'Rubbish, we are all civilians.' This proved too much for our man. A cow speaking with a human voice could not have impressed him more. 'Are you German?' he asked, with amazement written all over his bloated face.

'No, but I speak German,' said our man.

The *Feldwebel* recovered his composure. He stretched out his arm: 'Your papers.' Mr Burhardt had documents. We had none.

'You have a German name,' said the *Feldwebel* with a simile of a smile. A polite discussion followed on the origins of the Burhardt family, the time of their arrival in Poland, etc, etc. Moreover, Mr Burhardt's civilian trousers, with a hole at the site of his wound, seemed to confirm his non-combatant status. In fact he had just managed to get rid of his army trousers, which he had worn on top of the others.

In short, we were saved.

We stayed in the cellar for three days. The *Feldwebel* and his men kept visiting us. Their unit was a *Strafkompanie*, or a penal company consisting of the politically unreliable and other 'undesirables'. So much the better.

The *Feldwebel* himself, my would-be assassin, was a Rhinelander, the son of a hotelier. Our only common language was French which, being a frontiersman, he knew better than I. He didn't dare to write to his parents that he was fighting in Warsaw. He had been assigned to the penal company for having hit his lieutenant when he had found his French fiancée in bed with the officer. He was sent first to the Russian front and then transferred to the penal unit in Warsaw. Among our German visitors was also a Silesian, Romanowski, who spoke Polish. He was in the Army's bad books because of his suspect origin, I presume.

Unwashed for days, I was not conscious of my own smell – anyway, the cellar air was far from sweet – but I could feel the stubble on my chin. Time to shave, I thought to myself. The next German 'visitor' might shoot me just for my dirty face. And so I asked one of the soldiers to shave me. He applied himself to the task with gusto. I had to persuade him not to leave me a little goatee. And how full of sympathy he was! He was practically shedding tears over me, because his razor blade was blunt and he hated the thought that he might be hurting me. I gave him absolution. But this was the same man who the day before was shooting the wounded next door when ordered to do so by an officer.

Another German, somewhat embarrassed, returned to our cellar to collect the bunch of grenades he had left behind the day before. Gentlemen that we were, we returned his lost property to him.

Still another, slightly tipsy, sat on my pallet and said '*Schade, schade ich bin nicht Pole, ich wäre auch Partisan sein*, pity, pity I am not a Pole, I would also have been a partisan.'

Naturally, I protested vigorously: 'I am a civilian. I have never been a partisan.' He patted me on the shoulder and left.

At the time, Czerniaków was being shelled by Soviet artillery from across the Vistula. Eventually an order came to move the survivors into the open, into the courtyard of the house. By then only ten of us were left of the original hundred casualties treated in the hospital. After the long days in the cellar, the air in the courtyard felt reasonably fresh. The fire which had consumed the house next to ours was slowly dying down. Suddenly, groans reached us from there and a German officer sent two soldiers to investigate. Risking their lives, the men went into the smouldering ruin whose weakened timbers could have collapsed at any time. A minute later they carried out a Polish civilian. They brought him, barely alive, to the officer. 'Look at that,' the officer pointed to the creased right sleeve of the man's jacket. 'A sniper. Shoot him,' he ordered. The same two soldiers who had dragged him out of the burning house took the man to the side and shot him through the head. '*Befehl ist Befehl*, an order is an order,' is after all an old German maxim.

We were to be evacuated, but when? Where to? Suddenly, with no warning whatsoever, two Poles escorted by an armed German soldier were next to me putting me on a stretcher, and off we went, accompanied by an older man with a leg wound. It all happened so quickly that I did not even have time to say goodbye either to Irka or to the other nurse. From the stretcher carried at shoulder level I could not see the older man, but he seemed to be having problems keeping up with my two porters. The soldier shouted '*Schnell*, fast march!' And then I heard a rifle repeat, a shot, and *schnell* we went. The older man, not *schnell* enough, was dead.

We crossed the Ujazdowski Park next to the Military Hospital where I had been a patient before the war and where Stasinek and Jerzy had studied as army doctors. From my high perch on the stretcher I saw scattered containers which had been dropped several days back by allied planes. There they were, full of ammunition, dressings and food rations, with parachutes still attached – our badly needed supplies, delivered to the wrong address.

The planes, many with Polish crews, were starting from airports in Italy. The allies requested permission to land and refuel behind the front line, on Soviet-occupied territory. The request was refused. 'No available landing strips,' was the reason given by Stalin. And so the allied planes had to carry sufficient fuel for their return journey. Their payload was thus greatly reduced, as was the time allotted to finding the designated drop areas.

My stretcher trip ended in Szucha Avenue, where my porters deposited me on the pavement, in the shade of a tree and with a good view of the Gestapo headquarters across the street. This was the very building I had visited in October 1939 demanding my father's release; good God, was it only five years ago?! I was not alone. There were five more of our casualties on the pavement, including a girl with a huge dumdum chest wound.

This part of the capital, reserved for the Germans since the beginning of the occupation, had been left untouched by the recent fighting. On this particular afternoon, only two or three shells coming from the other side of the Vistula shattered the peace and after the last seven weeks of war in the ruins of Warsaw the silence was uncanny.

A Gestapo officer walking his dog stopped next to us. 'Where did they bring you from? Who are you?' he asked in perfect Polish.

'I am a civilian,' volunteered a teenager of perhaps sixteen or seventeen, stretched on the pavement next to me. 'Nobody had bothered about us, civilians,' he continued. 'Home Army soldiers alone were cared for . . .' I didn't like this prattle, almost a betrayal. The officer just shrugged his shoulders and left.

The night was already dark when we were moved into the Gestapo cellars which saw so many of my friends and countless others tortured, often to death. A doctor came in. He spoke a little Polish, but he re-dressed my wounds, no questions asked. Later in the night, an army ambulance took us to the Infant Jesus Hospital run by nuns. We were left alone in a dark entrance hall; there was no electricity. A clock sounded midnight.

Only the young boy and I survived the rest of the night. The following day the boy bled to death, and of all of us I alone remained among the living.

Later in the morning – it was either 25 or 26 September – I was moved into a ward, to a real bed. With not a glass pane left intact, the ward was cold. Soon rain was coming in and the beds had to be pushed away from the walls.

I was not well. My right arm was still paralysed. None of my wounds, either the ones sustained on 4 August or those dating to 31 August and 11 September, were healing. I kept trying to move the fingers of my right hand with the fully operational left one. By chance, I discovered that my right ring finger was bending in the wrong place, a centimetre above the joint. 'Yes,' confirmed the doctor, 'your finger is broken. We missed it.' He splinted the finger, but the bone didn't heal correctly and the finger is crooked to this day. One of my war mementoes.

Each change of dressings would take about an hour and I had to stay naked, while the ward temperature dropped to ten degrees centigrade or even five degrees centigrade. My abdominal wound healed by itself: one day the hole made by the shrapnel discharged a river of pus, like egg yolk. Apparently a metal splinter came with it, though I did not notice it. After a long break, my bodily functions returned. I cheated the doctors and survived.

In the overcrowded hospital the nuns were devilishly, if that's the right word, overworked. Food was, to say the least, scarce. It was invariably watery soup. A bowl of it would be placed on my chest and I was left to manage, eating it with my left hand. I took great care not to spill even one precious spoonful.

TWENTY

The Warsaw Rising 5: The Surrender
(2 October 1944)

ON 2 OCTOBER, NEWS SPREAD THROUGH THE HOSPITAL: the Rising had collapsed, we had surrendered, the insurgents would be taken to Germany as prisoners of war. At first I couldn't believe my ears, but in the next couple of days the end of the fighting was confirmed and re-confirmed. All the civilian inhabitants were ordered to quit the capital, leaving their belongings behind. Many would be deported to Germany as slave labour. Some of the trains would go, inexplicably, straight to Ravensbrück, one of the worst German concentration camps for women. This was to be the fate of Mrs Hetlinger, our neighbour in Żolibórz, the one who had warned me about the presence of Germans in our flat.

Much later I learned that the rest of my group in the Czerniaków Hospital, including Irka, were taken to Germany as prisoners of war. A German detachment had taken with them the other nurse, the pretty one, and she disappeared without trace. After the war Irka told me how she had been concerned for me, as after the evacuation of Czerniaków I was nowhere to be found.

Of my *Kedyw* friends Zosia, Danusia and, in spite of his wounds, Janek Bagiński managed to cross the Vistula. Kryst, unscathed, was mobilised into the Polish Army which was part of the Red Army, and fought in their ranks all the way to Berlin. Jerzy and several others made their way via sewers to Mokotów and after the surrender were also taken prisoner. Of my close circle of friends, Zosia alone emerged from those two months of hell without a single injury. Danusia had been seriously wounded on reaching the other side of the Vistula and was saved by Zosia, who single-handedly pulled her off the riverbank onto the embankment. Overall, *Kedyw* losses amounted to about seventy per cent dead. Sonka had beaten me in the number of wounds: while I had only three serious injuries and one minor one, he had been wounded seven times. Sadly, the seventh time proved fatal and he died of tetanus. Now, in my old age, I frequently reflect on the fate of my comrades who died such a violent death so young. My granddaughter is older now than many of them were at the time. In my mind I still see them in their teens and early twenties – our lost generation.

Let me now go back to my hospital bed. One day all the able-bodied, mostly relatives of patients, raided the abandoned German food stores. They returned with loads of flour and rancid butter. The women took to baking shortcakes for their kith and kin. Unfortunately, I had no relatives to look after me.

With nothing better to do, and with my paralysed right arm making writing difficult, I dictated to my neighbour a little poem dedicated to our ward sister, a sour-faced and very authoritarian nun. Unobtrusively, I presented it to her. The theme of my poem was simple: I am hungry and my dreams are full of shortcakes. At first nothing happened. Then in the darkness of the night I heard footsteps and a paper bag full of shortcakes gently landed on my chest. They were exquisite, even though they smelled of rancid butter. The moral: poetry can gain you cakes, not just your daily bread.

TWENTY-ONE

The 'Liberation': 17 January 1945.
Family Reunions

TIME WAS PASSING. I STARTED WALKING. My left foot was still very stiff, with the Achilles tendon in spasm and the ankle in permanent extension. I limped badly, but at least I was mobile again.

I'd had a bellyful of hospitals. It was time to leave. I knew that my mother was staying with Mrs Olewińska in Konstancin and I decided to join her. But the very thought of it seemed preposterous. How was I going to get there? There was no public transport of any kind. I had no documents, none at all. The Germans were still in control and being caught without valid papers meant either a summary execution or, at best, imprisonment and deportation to a concentration camp.

Somebody told me that the hospital director's son had taken part in the Rising and was killed in the Old City. Perhaps the father would prove sympathetic and willing to help. He listened to my story with great patience, and kept sadly shaking his head. Eventually, I left his office with an official-looking piece of paper bearing the hospital heading. It stated that Mr Henryk Wichowski – one of the names I was using at the time – had lost all his documents. The good doctor signed and stamped the paper. However, I had no photograph to attach to it and was fully aware that without my mug shot the document would not be valid in the eyes of the Germans.

One day I noticed an unusual commotion in the courtyard of the hospital. Loads of hospital equipment wrapped in sheets, rags and tarpaulins, including the X-ray apparatus, were being placed on to horse-drawn vehicles to be evacuated. Another cart, with several planks for seats, was being readied for the nuns. Not without difficulty, I climbed to the top of the mound of equipment, heaving my disobedient body some three metres up from the ground. I stayed there, stretched out precariously, holding on fast to a thick rope. No sooner had I secured my place than we were leaving the hospital and proceeding west.

Our destination was Grodzisk, a town about twenty kilometres south-west of Warsaw. The name sounded vaguely familiar. But where had I heard it? I racked my brains for a while, and suddenly it came to me. I had heard on the grapevine that Olek Tyrawski's family, evacuated from Żolibórz, had moved to Grodzisk. This might be my lucky break.

At the city boundary near the Warsaw West railway station there was a road block manned by German military police, some twenty of them in their *feldgrau* uniforms and steel helmets. 'Come down,' called the driver, 'Document control.' Special permits were required for leaving Warsaw and he had one for himself, his mate and the ten nuns. He must have assumed that I had one of my own. But with my worthless piece of paper, my goose was as good as cooked. 'I am staying here,' I said. 'They will have to get me down by force.' The driver understood. He kept mum and I stayed on top, glued to the pile of equipment, trying to shrink to invisibility. I must have succeeded – they didn't notice me.

We continued on our way at walking pace. The ride was far from comfortable, but even so I managed to snatch some sleep. It was amazing how I managed that without falling off my perch. I woke up two or three hours later, in Grodzisk.

I got word to the Tyrawski family. Jurek, Olek's brother, soon arrived to fetch me in a borrowed peasant cart. At last, I was in a friendly home where I was welcome and looked after along with Bogdan, Jurek's brother-in-law, who was seriously wounded with a splinter in his heart muscle; he is alive to this day, still carrying the piece of metal in his chest. Luckily, the Tyrawski family had saved my gold twenty-dollar coin, which I had entrusted to Olek at some stage. Suddenly I was rich; at the time the precious coin represented a small fortune and allowed me to buy the food which I so badly needed. Jurek's three-year-old daughter, Ewa, acted as my messenger. Every fifteen minutes, timing it exactly on the Cyma watch, a gift from my father in 1938, I would send Ewa out for a snack: a plateful of sweetened curd cheese, a buttered roll, a helping of egg yolks beaten with sugar. Fortunately I could afford these gastronomic orgies, but the self-imposed intervals between them seemed to go on forever.

When at last I managed to get a message to Mother that I was in

Grodzisk, she arrived, on foot . . . having walked all the twenty-five kilometres. Having first spied Bogdan in his bed, she screamed 'My son! My son!' and, before I managed to call from the next room 'I am here, Mother!' she fell on him, hugging him tightly and half-lifting him off his pillow.

Mother had never doubted that I would survive. In spite of the red glow of fires clearly visible over Warsaw night after night, in spite of the rumble of constant cannon-fire and the echoes of distant explosions reaching Konstancin, she had never had any misgivings about me coming back. My mother was not a worrier, she would never fantasize about what *might* happen. This character trait helped her to live to the ripe old age of ninety-five. And, true enough, her intuition never failed her.

My left leg continued to give me hell. It was, in fact, getting worse. I was taken in a peasant's horse-drawn cart some ten kilometres to the Infant Jesus Hospital, which had been evacuated from the ruins of Warsaw to Milanówek and which now had a working X-ray department. I was told that a large metal fragment had lodged in my left heel and caused *osteomyelitis*, or bone infection. Surgery was urgently required to remove the splinter and scrape out the bone.

The same cart took me to Konstancin where Dr Ambros, a surgeon of high repute, performed the operation. The hospital was in the converted 'Sans Souci' villa. Once in Konstancin, I felt at home. My old friends were coming to visit me in droves.

The operation was successful but the wound refused to heal: my old wounds were still stubbornly refusing to scar over, and the new one followed their example. Proud flesh proliferated everywhere, interfering with the normal healing process. At least this operation had been carried out under more civilised conditions than those I had been used to during the Rising. Ether was available and I felt no pain. However, during the induction of anaesthesia I had a curious experience. Just before going under I was overwhelmed by a feeling that I was dying. I felt I had to tell the doctor about it, but there was not enough time. This sensation of having died was so convincing that on waking up I was conscious of only one overwhelming thought: 'Had they cut off my head instead of scraping my bone it would have made no difference . . .' Ever since, I have imagined death to be such a simple process: just oblivion, no other worlds, no angels on fluffy clouds. And yet, not having actually died, I have not been able to prove it or to say to the believers: 'I know there is nothing, I have been there.' I have since had operations under anaesthetics other than ether, and never again have I had a similar sensation. But this peculiar experience has remained engraved on my memory and, though I am not in a hurry, I am still waiting for the final proof of my conviction.

❧

In the meantime, the German occupation continued. The front line ran six kilometres east of Konstancin along the Vistula. The dull rumble of artillery reached us day and night.

We were looked after by several nuns; the only one I remember is sister Ludwika, the youngest and prettiest of them. I was in a room with three other patients. One of them was a Ukrainian whose leg had been amputated. He was telling me about the collectivisation of Ukrainian villages ordered by Stalin in 1933 and the resulting famine which had caused the deaths of millions of peasant families. He had lived through it as a small boy, and now greatly feared the approaching Red Army. The Germans had forced him into their service and put him to digging trenches, making him an unwilling collaborator. The Russians were bound to treat him as a traitor and condemn him to death.

I remained bedridden. The surgeon reasoned that an upright posture, improving the blood supply to my legs, would result in the formation of more proud flesh, preventing proper healing. The doctors tried all kinds of treatment, but with no success. The operation was performed in November and I hoped to be discharged in time for Christmas, or at the latest early in the New Year of 1945, but the festive season came and went and I was still in hospital. Eventually, it was an old wives' remedy that brought me back to health. A woman friend suggested alternate foot baths in an infusion of camomile and a solution of potassium permanganate. Miraculously, after ten days of this treatment my heel was covered with a thin but normal skin. After two months in bed, I was once more up and about.

However, I was still bedridden when at long last the front had started moving again. The Red Army, including the Polish Division formed in the USSR, crossed the Vistula. Warsaw was captured on 17 January 1945. In the meantime, after the collapse of the Rising, i.e. during October and November 1944, the Germans, acting on Hitler's direct orders, wrought their wrath on the hapless city by systematically blowing up most of those buildings which dared to remain standing. By the time Warsaw fell to the Russians ninety per cent of the city was in ruins, many of the streets unidentifiable. Only some of the suburbs, Żolibórz among them, escaped.

Rumour had it that our hospital was to be evacuated by the Germans. I was still unable to walk. 'How are you going to get me out of here?' I asked Mother. 'You will see,' she said, unruffled as usual. 'Everything will be fine.' And again she was proved right. The Germans abandoned the area without a fight, leaving the hospital behind. Konstancin was in the path of the Polish units. Word reached me that one of their officers, I never found out who, kept asking the locals: 'Did the Likiernik family survive?' He was told by one of them: 'Yes, Mrs Likiernik lives at Mrs Olewińska's.' This was very revealing. Mother was ostensibly Mrs Malinowska, and her real name was supposed to be a closely guarded secret. In fact, all of Konstancin and its environs knew her true identity, but nobody had betrayed her to the Germans.

Soon, disturbing news started reaching us about the treatment meted out by our 'liberators' to members of the Home Army caught on the east side of the Vistula. Halinka was the one who told me about the persecutions, arrests and deportations to Siberia. This sounded so implausible that I refused to believe her – until, three days into our 'liberation', a new patient was admitted to the hospital. He was Tadeusz Kozłowski, an old friend of mine from the pre-war Konstancin days. He had been recognised as a member of the Home Army and severely beaten by well-known local thugs, now miraculously transformed into 'militiamen' of the new communist regime.

I was now up and about, but once again I had nothing to wear. At least this time arrangements were made for a tailor to come to the hospital; he took my measurements while I was still in bed, and managed to procure for me a pair of trousers, a jacket and an overcoat. Thus dressed and still limping, in March 1945 I was at long last able to leave hospital for good. But I had no idea what to do next.

First of all, I decided to find out what happened to our home in Warsaw and to the cache in Płachtowskis' flat. It wasn't until May 1945 that I managed to get to Warsaw. Our concrete-built apartment block in Żolibórz was still standing, and though the ground and first floors had been destroyed by fire, the second and third floors remained intact. Our third floor flat, which between 4 February 1944 and the end of the war had been occupied by a *Volksdeutsche* (a Pole of German descent who opted for the status of a German), now stood empty and devastated. To fit it out from scratch would have been virtually impossible. This fact had far-reaching consequences. Had I gone to Warsaw several weeks earlier, I might have found the flat habitable, equipped by the German tenant, fit to be taken over. This might have encouraged us to stay in Warsaw for good and life would have taken a different course. The cache in the Płachtowskis' flat was empty, except for a few photographs of no interest to the thieves. I took them and treasure them to this day.

❧

I vividly remember the day of 8 May 1945. I was standing with a comrade from the Home Army at the corner of Nowy Świat and Aleje Jerozolimskie when loudspeakers announced the surrender of Germany and the end of the war. This was the news we had longed for all those unending years, but when it came, it found us far from happy. The Germans had gone, but their place was taken by the Russians. We were not allowed to forget it, not for a moment. Every piece of wall still standing in Warsaw was now covered with huge posters showing a magnificent Soviet warrior, a Russian sub-machine gun across his chest, with a Polish Home Army soldier in the shape of a hunchbacked dwarf cowering at his feet. To add realism to this portrayal the Pole was depicted with globs of spit on his face, while the words: 'The Spit-covered Dwarf of Capitalism' underlined the meaning for those of no imagination. Was this to be the free and independent Poland we had fought so hard for?

TWENTY-TWO

After the War.
The Polish People's Republic

NOW, FROM THE PERSPECTIVE OF MORE THAN FIFTY YEARS, one could conclude that this period marked the end of the most difficult time of my life. In addition to the scars imprinted on my body, those five years of tribulations left indelible marks on my psyche. I had discovered the meaning of friendship, of solidarity, the pricelessness of team effort. One could not have risked one's life, repeatedly, without the motto of 'all for one and one for all' deeply engraved on one's mind and heart. I had witnessed scenes of inhuman behaviour by men who sank below the level of wild beasts. God – if he existed – had no right to allow these abominations. My loss of faith was justified once again.

Paradoxically, the collective slavery imposed by the enemy gave many of us, including myself, a feeling of an unaccustomed individual freedom. True enough, this freedom was relative but at times nevertheless I felt it very keenly, some of the constraints of orderly society having disappeared. The conviction has never left me that those who strive to impose their will on others are beyond the pale, villains with no place in the society of man.

The transition to normal life was difficult. At first I didn't know where to start. I had a clandestine vocational school's certificate in chemistry, and resolved to continue in that line at university level. To complete my *Matura*, the full peace-time matriculation certificate, I needed a pass in Polish language and literature, which I decided to sit for. This meant a lot of work.

A new university, which included a faculty of chemistry, opened in Lódz. With Warsaw destroyed beyond recognition and its remaining population expelled, Lódz, an industrial town situated about 150 kilometres south-west of Warsaw, which by comparison had suffered very little, now became the unofficial capital of Poland. Many people expelled from Warsaw had settled there and when I learned that Ata Branicka-Rybińska with her husband, Lech, and Remec now lived in Lódz, in the house once belonging to the Aronsons, Rysiek's parents, I decided to join them.

I had met Rysiek in *Kedyw*. His parents, rounded up by the Germans, died in Auschwitz. He survived by jumping from the train taking them to the camp and was saved by a peasant farmer. Helped by friends, he managed to find his way into our clandestine world and eventually joined *Kedyw*, the Warsaw-South unit. We had taken part in a few joint actions, but I only got to know him well in the first few days of the Rising when *Kedyw* regrouped. I lost sight of him again on the fourth day after being wounded. Rysiek then fought in the Old City, and in one of the incidents at the Pfeiffer tannery was wounded in the chest and leg. He was one of the patients saved by Remec's ruse of acting the part of a priest.

Now Rysiek had reclaimed the big house in Lódz his parents had owned and opened it to his friends. I joined the crowd. There was one unusual member of the household – his father's cousin, a Palestinian Jew and a volunteer in the British Army. Not counting the ubiquitous Russians, Rysiek's exotic relative was the only Allied soldier in Lódz and, in his British battledress, the darling of the town: particularly of the ladies.

On joining the household I was introduced to yet another inmate, a dapper man of about sixty. My surname aroused his curiosity. 'Likiernik?' he asked. 'A long time ago, before 1914, I used to know a Tadeusz Likiernik. He was a frequent visitor in *Oaza*, the Warsaw night club, and would often buy champagne for the whole company. Would you know him by any chance?'

'Yes, he happens to be my father.'

'Oh, I am sorry if I offended you,' said the man. But I didn't mind in the least. I had never heard this particular story, but I did know that between the death of my grandfather in 1911 and the start of the First World War in 1914, my father revelled away most of the family's fortune. Not that I blame him for it. It would have all been lost during that war anyway. He might as well have enjoyed it.

At the end of the Rising and our war, the Home Army still had some money left in the kitty and I arrived in Lódz with ten US dollars demobilisation allowance in my pocket. At the time, this was a considerable sum. My heritage telling, with gay abandon I spent it in less than a month. One day I realised my pocket was empty and asked one of my companions for a two złoty tram fare. 'You'll have to walk, you should not have thrown your money away,' he said, even though I had paid for his dinner the night before. I have never forgotten the lesson.

My lack of political nous led me to a sticky pass on Labour Day, 1 May 1945. In the People's Republic of Poland this was of course a national holiday and Remec, who had a proper job, had to march with the staff of his workplace in a solemn procession. And so the rest of us went to Piotrkowska Street, the main street of Łódz, to see the parade. In spite of the rain, the street was crowded. We managed to find a place in the first row of onlookers. 'Who may all those greybeards be?' I asked jokingly, pointing at the huge posters bearing the faces of Marx, Engels, Lenin and other luminaries. 'What a pity,' I continued, 'that our young socialists have to march in their raincoats. Their blue shirts and red ties would look so much more picturesque.'

In my naivety, I continued in this vein for a while until I felt a gentle tap on my shoulder. A man in a black leather coat stood close behind me. 'Follow us,' he said curtly, pointing discreetly to a soldier behind him. There was nothing for it, we had to comply. They took us, the entire small group, to a villa several streets away. It looked like any ordinary villa. There was no signboard, no notice of any sort. But it had to be some kind of police station. Polish political police? Or Russian?

We were told to wait and, to our surprise, were left together in one room. This was a hopeful sign. Then we were called one by one to see an officer. 'What exactly,' he asked me, 'did you say there, at the Labour Day parade?' I decided to play the fool, and faithfully repeated my own words, which he must have known already. 'Until my friends told me, I had no idea whose faces those were on the placards. Marx and Engels,' I said wonderingly. 'Nice faces, intelligent,' I added for good measure. 'I was also really sorry that these fine young people had to march with their raincoats on. But it was understandable in all that rain. They could have caught a cold, or even pneumonia. My mother would have my guts for garters if I dared to go out without a raincoat in weather like that.'

The police officer seemed to be swallowing all the rubbish I was spouting. Or perhaps he just pretended. But then he asked, sort of innocently, whether I had by any chance been a member of the Home Army. 'Of course not,' I said. 'My mother would never have let me. I would not even have dared to ask her permission.'

He seemed to swallow this as well. 'One never knows,' he added.

'In the AL (The People's Army – the communist underground),' he continued, 'I had a comrade whose friend was in the AK.'

'What a disgrace!' I exclaimed. This new Polish political police officer would not have been nearly so shocked had his chum's friend been an SS man.

He must have concluded that after all we were not 'Spit-covered dwarfs of the Capitalist Home Army' and let us all go. Another lucky escape. The most likely alternative would have been a trip to Siberia for a long period of re-education.

To enter the Faculty of Chemistry, I had to sit an entrance examination. The lady examiner had the temerity to ask me the chemical composition of raw rubber. I didn't have the faintest idea. My career as an industrial chemist abruptly came to an end. And so did my stay in Lódz.

Some time before I left the city, Honorata came to Lódz with a message from her boss, Rybicki. He invited us to join him in further clandestine activity, this time against the Soviet occupant. But most of us refused. We'd had enough, a bellyful of this game. Soon after, Rybicki was arrested and tortured. The organisation disintegrated. I heard his story later from his own mouth. In the middle of winter they had kept him in a cell with glassless windows, from time to time soaking him in cold water. He suffered a recurrence of bone tuberculosis, first contracted as a complication of wounds sustained in the 1920 Polish–Bolshevik war. Eventually they let him go home temporarily, on health grounds. He could have been released for good on the condition that he renounced, in writing, all political activity. He sought his wife's advice, but she did not think it was up to her to influence his decision. He refused to sign the renunciation paper and returned to prison, not knowing what his sentence was going to be.

In 1956, when the coming to power of Gomółka was followed by a partial relaxation of the Stalinist regime, Rybicki was released. Only then did he discover that he had been sentenced to many years imprisonment. Even after his release from prison, throughout the communist period, he remained under surveillance and his villa in Milanówek was repeatedly raided and searched by the political police.

When I first went to Warsaw after the war, I returned to our old flat in Żolibórz and found some words scribbled on the wall next to the main door. They were simply '*Wacek Koc*' and an address. I cannot describe my feeling of relief and joy: Wacek was alive! He had survived the concentration camp! I learned later that from

Buchenwald he had been moved to prison in Bytom, Silesia, where he was meant to serve as witness in the case of a Ukrainian guard accused of theft in a Lwów prison. Even so near to the end of the war, with the Red Army virtually on the doorstep, German bureaucracy was still as efficient as ever. In this prison the captives were divided into two classes: political prisoners and criminals. Fortunately Wacek managed to get himself classified as a criminal, as all the politicals were eventually executed.

The address I found on the wall was in Sopot, on the Baltic seaside. I decided to join Wacek there. The railways were just about operational and, with a bottle of vodka as a bribe, I got a place in the mail car. With the nearby Gdynia (a Polish port built in the 1920s and '30s) and Gdańsk (better known in the West by its German name of Danzig), Sopot had become part of a conurbation. The journey from Warsaw was long and tedious. However, I had company: a non-commissioned officer of the NKVD (Soviet political police) was travelling in the same car. I tried to be friendly. 'At long last the war is finished,' I said in my broken Russian.

'*Vsyo ravno*, it makes no difference to me,' was his curt reply.

'But you might have been killed,' I insisted.

'*Vsyo ravno*,' he repeated. 'There are so many of us . . .'

This was the end of the conversation. Obviously that kind of mentality was one of the factors responsible for the huge Soviet losses during the war. At one point Kryst, one of the *Kedyw* fraternity, told me that the Russians knew only one command: '*V peryod*, forward!' When talking to them, he could never make them see that there are situations when it might be preferable to knock out a tank with a petrol bottle thrown from a window or a roof rather than attempt a frontal attack. Yet Stalin did not care about casualties. In his deals with Churchill and Roosevelt, he used the argument of the great Soviet losses to his advantage; the more men he lost, the stronger was his argument.

I lived in Sopot as if in a dream. Halina, Zosia's sister, and Irena, another young woman I had met in the past in Żolibórz, had settled in an abandoned German villa and offered me their spare room. I decided I deserved a month's holiday. The weather was sunny and hot. I spent my days on the beach enjoying myself, resting and swimming. Irena, who worked in the Red Cross, arranged access to the canteen for me, where the soup was good and very filling.

After my holiday, I started work in the Planning Department of the Gdynia – Gdańsk Port Reconstruction Bureau, in September 1945. I got this job with the help of Colonel Pohowski, one of the

Bureau's employees, who happened to have been Wacek's superior officer in the Underground. The personnel officer, lately a soldier of the presently proscribed Home Army, was now disguised as a member of the Polish Workers' (i.e. Communist) Party. In fact, all the employees of our department were former Home Army members from Lwów.

In addition to my job, I managed to continue my education. I first registered at the Department of Chemistry of the Gdańsk Technological Institute but, mindful of my failure in Lódź, I soon changed direction. I learned of the forthcoming opening of the School of Maritime Trade in Gdynia and decided to apply. Our examiner in English happened to be Lena, my teacher of English in Warsaw. Now married, Mrs Lena Mahut lived in Sopot. Coming across her certainly improved my chances of passing the entrance exam. I had met Lena about a year before the Rising, when I was trying to learn English. She was about two or three years my senior. In addition to Polish she was fluent in Russian, German, French and English. She came from an assimilated Jewish family but, not having Jewish facial features, she found shelter on the so-called Aryan side of Warsaw with some family friends. She had been teaching me English for several months. At that time my experience of women was very limited, and I had no idea that she found me attractive. When I missed some lessons without forewarning her, she naturally assumed that I had either been arrested or killed. On returning after a two-weeks' absence, I found her so emotional that it made me think . . .

Soon after the Rising Lena met Mr Mahut, married him and eventually settled in Sopot. I was delighted to renew my friendship with Lena; her husband and I became good friends. Before long I moved in with them to a flat near the centre of Sopot. My mother, who had nothing to keep her in Warsaw now, also came to the seaside and I found her a bedsitter close to us.

When the academic term started, I would work in the office from 8 a.m. to noon and attend lectures in the afternoon. I found an old abandoned motorcycle and was forever trying to repair it. I applied to our personnel officer for a flat for Mother and myself. Life took on a semblance of normality. I was seeing Wacek frequently. He was working in an army-run film unit, a job he secured with the help of a certain Mr Spychalski. This man had been his mother's tenant during the war, when he worked in the communist underground. Now a communist general, he remembered Wacek's mother with fondness and gratitude and was glad to help her son.

Sopot was full of former inhabitants of Warsaw. Many of us had only known each other by sight, but now we became one big family, long-lost reunited friends. At the time a new nostalgic song came into fashion: 'Warsaw, oh, my dear old Warsaw.' It would have been sacrilege to dance to this tune. Even in night clubs and dancing halls, we would stop and listen to it with reverence.

I remember the wonderful 1945–46 New Year's Eve in the Mahuts' flat. We danced all night. At dawn, we were still welcoming the New Year at the far end of the pier, with snow up to our ankles.

I had no foreboding that this would be my last New Year's Eve in Poland.

TWENTY-THREE

To Freedom Across Europe

ONE DAY TOWARDS THE END OF JANUARY 1946, I returned home from a stroll in the Gdańsk harbour with Mr Mahut's attractive young sister to find a brief note from Wacek. It simply said: 'I've got to see you immediately. I'll be leaving Sopot on the 1430 Warsaw train.' This message changed the course of my life.

I ran all the way to the station and reached the platform just as the train was moving off. I managed to jump in and travelled to the next station so that I could talk to Wacek. The train was crowded, but we found a quiet spot in the corridor. I was still catching my breath when Wacek said quietly in my ear, 'My father is in France. And so is yours. I've heard it directly from an emissary of the Polish Army in the West. Edmund put me in touch with him.' He stopped and looked at me as if to check whether the significance of what he said had sunk in. It had. Edmund was Wacek's brother-in-law and an old friend of mine. I quickly examined the faces of the other passengers around us. They could not possibly overhear us over the clatter of the speeding train. Eager to hear more, I waited for Wacek to continue. 'The contact gave me an address in Cieszyn. These people would help me to slip across the Czech border. I am to proceed to Pilsen and report there to the Military Mission of the Polish Government-in-Exile in London.'

I couldn't believe my ears. It all sounded too good to be true. Wacek must have read my thoughts. 'They have it all worked out,' he continued, and then looked at me. 'I am going. What about you?'

There was no time for hesitation. 'I am coming with you,' I said. We agreed to meet in two days' time in Katowice, a town fairly close to Cieszyn.

In fact, the thought of leaving for the West had been growing in my mind for some time, but only as a vague idea. Several days before our conversation I had had a very odd experience, a kind of revelation. I was in the street, walking along, when I came face-to-face with another 'me' and looked at myself as if from the outside, as a passer-by might have done. There I was, opposite myself, waiting for something to happen. But what? Time was moving inexorably, life was slipping by like a fast-flowing river and I was doing nothing to control its direction . . . The next moment, as I returned to the here-and-now, I was startled by the realisation that I could not arrest the flow of time and that if I did not regain control of my destiny, I could spend the rest of my life as an observer. Wacek's suggestion therefore fell on fertile soil.

When I presented the plan to Mother, she didn't have any doubts. 'Yes, certainly,' she said, 'go with Wacek. Find Father and decide with him whether he, or both of you, will be coming back or not.' She then gave me her gold wedding ring and I left her an enlarged photograph of myself, which hangs in my study to this day.

I met Wacek in Katowice as arranged. We proceeded to Cieszyn together, and on arrival Wacek went in search of our guide-to-be. He was back soon. Something had gone wrong. Either the address he had been given was incorrect, or something had happened in the meantime. Perhaps the contact had been blown. The police were called, and only by the skin of his teeth had he escaped falling into their hands. We had to leave Cieszyn post-haste and seek another route.

I remembered hearing that the Rybińskis, Ata and Lech, had moved from Lódz to Kraków and had just had their first baby. We decided to look them up. They were happy to see us, and gave us the address of Jerzy, our *Kedyw* doctor who, expelled from Warsaw, had temporarily settled in Katowice. We retraced our steps and went back to the Silesian capital. When we disclosed our intentions, Jerzy gave us the address of friends of his in Kudowa Zdrój. 'Just mention my name,' he reassured us. Kudowa Zdrój was a health resort very close to the Czech border.

We reached Kudowa Zdrój in the evening, were made welcome by Jerzy's friends and spent the night there. They were absolutely convinced that we were emissaries of the Home Army, and wouldn't accept our denials. Perhaps we didn't try that hard. Anyway, they did their best to help us. After some deliberation, they directed us to a forester's cottage close to the frontier. The forester was friendly and very generous. He gave us each a pair of skis, pointed us in the right direction and wished us Godspeed. There was nothing else he could do.

It was bitterly cold, some fifteen or twenty degrees centigrade of frost. We'd been on our feet for hours, skiing along the snow-covered track. It was February, and it was growing dark quite early in the afternoon. We thought of stopping for the night in the Socialist Youth Ski Hostel in Grünenwald which the forester had told us about, but we gave up the idea. The night was closing in and the temperature was dropping fast. In spite of the glare of the snow, by 5 p.m. it was pitch-dark. At last we came upon an isolated house. Taking a chance, we knocked. Once. Twice. No response for a long time. Then a woman's voice, in German, the tone not very inviting. 'Who is there? The owners are out. I cannot let you in.'

'But we shall freeze to death. Do help us. *Bitte.*'

A young woman opened the door, looked us up and down and let us in. The house was spacious, well heated. The German woman was alone with her two-year-old son. Her husband hadn't come back from the war. She put us up in a very comfortable room, and even offered us a hot bath. We could hardly believe our luck. It was like a dream. Some time later, another girl joined us unexpectedly from another flat in the house. Her husband was in hospital after an accident. This girl was very reserved to begin with but, evidently deprived of human contact for some time, she was soon eager to talk. She confirmed that the owners of the place were away. We concluded that she must be in hiding, though we've never found out why.

Washed, fed and rested, we awaited the return of the owners. Two young men appeared at about 8 p.m. They didn't even pretend to believe that we had been looking for the Socialist Youth Ski Hostel. 'If you want to cross the border,' said the older one, 'We can help you. It'll cost you five hundred złotys. We would have to leave at 6 a.m. The border is no problem to us. We have Polish documents in one pocket and Czech ones in the other,' he laughed uproariously. In the post-war muddle they had managed to get the two sets of documents; they also spoke fluent Polish and Czech.

We went to bed feeling very pleased with ourselves. Suddenly, at about 1 a.m., we woke up to insistent knocks on the main door. The door creaked open. Loud footsteps followed . . . heavy boots . . . the metallic clatter of guns. Had we been betrayed?

Quiet conversation reached us from the next room, then laughter and the clinking of glasses: '*Na zdrowie,* your health.' Heavy footsteps again. The main door opened and banged close. Once more all was quiet. After an anxious half-hour, we regained confidence in our guides. It had been a border patrol. They were looking for a warm fire and a glass of vodka; the temperature outside had dropped to minus twenty-five degrees centigrade.

In the morning, again on skis and wearing our city clothes, we followed our guides. The border ran along a mountain ridge and we faced a five-hundred-metre climb. Wacek was totally exhausted. It was only later that I learned that prison and the concentration camp had left him with a large tuberculous cavity in one lung.

We reached the top and started a steep descent to the other side. Our guides were professionals. I was keen on the sport, but Wacek had never been a skier. He proceeded gingerly from one tree to the next, clinging to each one for dear life. Under other circumstances it might have been a funny sight, at least for the rest of us, if not for poor Wacek. Eventually we made it. We left our skis behind and, escorted by our guides, we walked to Nachod. Once there, they bought us bus tickets to Hradec Králové and train tickets from there to Prague. They tried to provoke us into an admission that we were emissaries of the Underground, but we said neither yea nor nay. We parted company cordially, leaving our guides satisfied that they had helped two clandestine couriers on their way.

We reached Prague without difficulty. Up to 1948, Czecho-slovakia was a more-or-less liberal democracy governed by President Benes. Nevertheless, at the railway station police patrols were on the lookout for German refugees and illegal passengers. People were being stopped and their documents checked. Wacek had a Buchenwald inmate's certificate, in somebody else's name and without a photograph. I had a worthless piece of paper entitling me to search for my family. With every successive patrol coming into view, I hastened to hide in the station toilet. On my fifth visit to that establishment the female attendant commiserated with me. Wearing a suitably painful expression on my face, I appeared to suffer in silence. Without the language I could not talk to her, but she may have attributed my reticence to my evident discomfort.

At last the Pilsen train rolled slowly into the station. Fortunately, Czechs are not nearly as chatty as Poles and, at least in our compartment, people kept themselves to themselves. By keeping our mouths shut we could pass for natives. In Pilsen we went directly to the Polish Mission, whose address we had been given along with the name of the man in charge. But we were out of luck. The officer who had been informed to expect our arrival had just left for the station to catch the Munich train. It was scheduled to leave the Pilsen station in half an hour's time. We dashed back to the station. We ran from compartment to compartment – fortunately it was a very short train – and managed to find our Polish lieutenant. 'Go back to the mission,' he said. 'I'll return in four or five days' time and shall do what I can for you.'

We jumped off the train at the last minute. Neither Wacek nor I liked the idea of wasting time waiting for the lieutenant to return. Another train going towards the German border was about to depart. After a short 'war council', Wacek and I boarded it.

We got out at Folmowe, the last station before the frontier. It was 7 p.m., and the darkness of the winter night was broken only by a few dim lights. In the station hall we came across a group of young American soldiers, the first Americans we'd ever met. At the time my English was better than Wacek's – later, when he became a professor at Lancaster University, the position changed in his favour – and, as no more trains were expected, I suggested that they join us on a march to the German border. Naturally, I omitted to tell them that their company would make our crossing safer. 'What! Twelve kilometres! Over eight miles! On foot?!' They were genuinely amazed by my proposal. We set off on our own.

After no more than 200 metres of our lonely march along the railway track we were stopped by a Czech railwayman. After a short exchange of greetings, he said: 'Be careful. If it is the border you are aiming for, you are bound to be stopped by a brutal German guard posted there by the Americans. He hates us all, Czechs and Poles alike. What he'll do is lock you up for several days in a cellar and when you are half dead with cold and starvation, he will hand you in to the Czech authorities, who will in turn pass you to the Polish police.'

This was a timely warning. We left the railway track and made our way across ploughed fields towards a few faint lights glimmering in the distance. It was heavy going. At times the lights would disappear and so would our sense of direction. We were wandering blindly but eventually, by a circuitous route, we reached a little town called Furth-im-Wald. Somehow, without realising it we had slipped across the border!

The night was dark, we were cold and hungry and we had to look for shelter. We had been warned that the Americans returned Czech refugees caught in Germany back to the Czech authorities. This sounded implausible. They couldn't possibly do that to us, one a former concentration camp inmate and the other a Warsaw insurgent, a comrade-in-arms, so to speak. So we went straight to the American barracks. But they were unguarded and empty. In vain did we shout 'Hello, hello!' up and down the long corridors. Just as well, as we learned later that the Americans would have had no qualms about deporting fellow combatants back across the border.

We decided to try our luck elsewhere. I knocked on the first door we came to. 'We would like to rent a room for the night,' said Wacek in German.

'There is a dormitory for refugees in the school house,' the answer reached us through the closed door.

We found the school. Straw spread on the floor converted the classrooms into dormitories. We woke in the morning amidst a crowd of refugees: they were all Germans expelled or escaping from Czechoslovakia.

'Where do you come from? Are you *Volksdeutsche*, German nationals?'

'We are Polish.'

'What?!'

'Next time we shall finish off your lot for good!'

'Every fucking Czech, Pole, every bloody Slav!'

'Just you wait and see, we'll be attacking the USSR again soon, this time together with the Americans.' Threats were coming from all sides.

'I am a soldier of the SS. Not for nothing did the Americans release me from the prisoner-of-war camp,' a young boy, no more than seventeen or eighteen years of age, added with pride.

I couldn't restrain myself any longer. 'There's only one thing you understand: tra . . . ra . . . ra . . . ra . . .' With my hand providing the best possible imitation of a machinegun, I had them all in my sights.

Without further ado we opened our bags, reached for our bread and bacon and proceeded with our breakfast. This was our revenge. They had not seen or smelled bacon since God knows when. We chewed slowly, purposefully, tasting every morsel, making the smell waft round the room. Needless to say, we shared not a crumb with our neighbours.

On leaving Poland we took several thousand German marks with us. They were going cheap, but the transaction was risky: we couldn't be sure that they were still in circulation. Fortunately they were, so we were able to buy railway tickets to Munich. For some reason the train stopped in Ragensburg. There we met a troop of American soldiers manning the station army post. Once again I tried to forge good comrades-in-arms relations, but the young American who jabbered incomprehensibly in what was supposed to be Polish didn't share my good intentions, and we were unceremoniously shown the door before a dialogue could be established. I felt hurt and disheartened.

In Munich we at last found another Military Mission of the

Polish Government-in-Exile. In the doorway we ran into a young woman, an acquaintance from Żolibórz. I discovered later that her main function was to keep the head of the Mission, a Captain Świerczyński, happy. The latter made us welcome and gave us passes to Murnau, a town some fifty kilometres south of Munich in the direction of the Alps. He told us to report to the Polish camp there. We had no idea what to expect in Murnau. The existence there of an Oflag, or prisoner-of-war camp for Polish officers, was a surprise to us. The first of several surprises, in fact. Many of the ex-prisoners were still there.

We reported to the duty officer. He recorded our names, dates of birth and army ranks, and then turned to me 'You'll find your bed in block A and Mr Koc goes to block C.'

'But we want to stay together,' I protested vigorously.

'Impossible,' he said indignantly. 'You are a second lieutenant and Mr Koc is not an officer.' I have kept the lodging slips to this day as souvenirs.

This was not the welcome we had hoped for. However, we had more reporting to do. At the end of a long corridor we found two doorplates: 'Colonel X, Chief of Staff and Colonel Y, Deputy. Colonel X was thirsty for news and had evidently had little contact with new arrivals from Poland; he kept enquiring about our travels, about the general situation in the country and about the movements of the Soviet Army, though we had little information about the latter. 'What are your plans?' he eventually asked.

'We want to get to Paris and find both our fathers.'

'Very well. I'll write to Paris straight away and ask them to arrange study grants and visas for you. You must have visas,' he stressed.

'How long will that take, Colonel Sir?'

'Hopefully, not more than six months.'

'Thank you very much, Colonel Sir,' we said in unison, about turned and left. Without even discussing it, we went back to the railway station. Lose another six months! He had to be joking.

The journey back to Munich took longer than expected; there was some problem on the line. We arrived too late. The Mission was shut. To spend the night in the station was too risky: the American Military Police patrols kept checking for contraband, goods of American origin in general and cigarettes in particular. We had a few packets of those from Poland, to use for barter in case our marks proved worthless. I was by now weary of our 'allies' and of their Military Police in particular.

Captain Świerczyński had his quarters in a very large house standing in the middle of a park. This time he received us with obvious bad grace. 'What do you want? You should have reached Murnau by now.' He wouldn't accept our explanation. Shelter for the night? Out of the question. 'No room for you to sleep here.'

But his orderly stood to attention. 'Perhaps here, Captain Sir,' he dared to suggest, opening the door to a dormitory containing five made-up and empty beds. The captain was furious, but could not deny the evidence of spare accommodation.

In the morning, realising that he would not get rid of us in any other way, he wrote out a preposterous 'pass' for both of us on one scrap of paper. All it said was that we had lost our documents. 'You'll have to get into the French zone of occupation,' he said. 'In Ettlingen, south of Karlsruhe, you'll find a Polish camp where they will help you get to Paris.'

He was right about that. The Ettlingen Poles proved friendly and helpful. They added a French version to our 'pass', plus another rubber stamp. Our scrap of paper was beginning to look a little more official. They also provided us with passes to Baden-Baden, the administrative centre of the French occupation zone in Germany. At least we would be closer to our destination. Only one more border to cross!

Having arrived in Baden-Baden, we went first to the Military Mission of the London Polish Government. We were cordially received by its head, a certain Captain Kopa. However, he couldn't help us cross this last frontier. He was far too busy: what with coffee beans in occupied Germany being worth their weight in gold! Several kilograms of coffee would buy one a car. And while the latter could be obtained in Germany, coffee was easily available in France, where cars were not. No wonder Captain Kopa had very little time for us.

In addition to the Military Mission of the Polish Government-in-Exile, Baden-Baden also hosted a Military Mission of the Polish Government in Warsaw. We decided to try our luck there. At the time Poland could boast of two governments, both claiming legitimacy: one in exile in London, with its constitutional roots in the pre-war Polish state, the other in Warsaw, imposed by the Soviet 'liberators' and trying hard to acquire legitimacy by accepting into the cabinet Stanisław Mikołajczyk, hitherto a member of the government-in-exile.

In the Warsaw Military Mission we were received by a very attractive lady who, however, didn't speak any Polish. She was

Canadian, the wife of captain Dunin-Żupański. We managed to explain our situation in French. Her husband happened to be in Paris and she expected his return later that evening. 'You'd better come back tomorrow morning,' she advised. What about lodgings for the night? The duty officer in charge of quartermaster affairs was a lieutenant. 'What am I to do with you?' he exclaimed on seeing our papers. But in view of my officer rank, he assigned us to a room in one of the elegant Baden-Baden hotels. This establishment, built in the nineteenth century, still smacked of the *grande époque*. We spent the night in two huge beds in a luxurious bedroom – a reception worthy of the magnificent West. However, by morning the lieutenant had changed his mind and made us move to a hotel housing displaced persons, at the other end of the scale.

The result of our morning visit to Captain Żupański's office was satisfactory. He knew Wacek's surname well and mine even better. 'Last night in Paris,' he said, 'I met captain Szczerba-Likiernik. Any relation?'

'Very much so,' I said. 'My father's brother.'

'Very well,' he decided. 'I'll help you, but before 6 p.m. you are to report to me in Polish uniforms. 'I will get you passes for a furlough in Paris, but the passes have to be stamped by the French Military Security and their offices close at 6 p.m.'

The rest of the day was crazy. By chance we found a Polish tailor, a certain Mr Zawadzki, who had lived in Germany for forty years but still spoke good Polish and was glad to be of service. Through him we managed to find an American uniform. The trouble was that its original owner must have been 190 centimetres tall, and so a good deal taller than I. The top came down to my knees and when rolled up exposed my civilian trousers, over which I wore newly acquired pale-green summer uniform drill trousers. Everything was much too big, but it would have to do. Later, in an overheated railway car, I felt much too hot wearing two layers of clothes.

Wacek procured a military overcoat and altered it himself for size; he was expert in everything. We did not have the red 'POLAND' shoulder tabs, but the Military Mission supplied those. In the evening, issued with proper travel orders, we bought tickets for Paris. What's more, as soldiers going on leave we only had to pay a quarter of the normal fare.

Another great disappointment awaited me in the train. I was under the impression that my French was passable, but a French soldier from Marseilles shared our compartment and while he never stopped talking, I didn't understand a single word. It was his regional accent, as I now know, but he might have been speaking Chinese as far as I was concerned. At 6 a.m. we arrived in the Gare de l'Est. We were in Paris!

TWENTY-FOUR

Paris – Another World

BEFORE LEAVING POLAND I HAD LEARNED FROM MY AUNT, Alina Wojecka, that my uncle Kazimierz (Kazik for short) Szczerba-Likiernik, who was her and my father's brother, was in Paris, staying in Hôtel Lemoine. And so, on 8 February at 8 a.m., Wacek and I presented ourselves at the hotel's reception desk.

I did not know Kazik all that well; what I knew was mostly what my father had told me about his brother, ten years his junior. At the age of eighteen, at the start of the First World War in 1914, Kazik joined the Polish Legion commanded by Józef Piłsudski. The Legion fought on the side of the Central Powers against Russia, considered the principal oppressor and enemy of Poland. As he was born in the Russian-occupied part of Poland and was therefore the Tsar's subject, if taken prisoner by the Russians he would have been shot as a traitor. After Poland regained its independence in 1918, the Legion provided the nucleus of the Polish Army and Piłsudski, its creator and commanding officer, became the head of state. As was then common practice, Kazik retained his legionnaire *nom de guerre* of Szczerba, so that his surname became the double-barrelled Szczerba-Likiernik.

In the late 1930s, in addition to running a business, he was the Honorary Consul of Peru in Warsaw and, in the early summer of 1939, left Poland intending to spend several months in South America. The outbreak of the Second World War found him in Peru and, being a reserve officer of the Polish army in the rank of captain, he considered it his duty to return home and join a fighting unit. But at the time the long voyage by ship was the only way of getting across the Atlantic. By the time he reached France, Poland had already been overrun by the Germans and Russians. Consequently, he joined one of the units of the Polish Army being then reorganised in France under General Sikorski.

Wounded in Alsace, Kazik was taken prisoner by the Germans and spent the remaining years of the war in a German Oflag. After the war he was appointed Deputy Military Attaché of the Polish Embassy in Paris, now representing the new Polish Government in Warsaw. In spite of his leftist political sympathies, he didn't last long there.

Now back to that morning in Paris. The Hôtel Lemoin porter seemed a bit embarrassed by our request to see my uncle. 'You see, he is not alone,' he said. 'You'd better wait here and I'll tell him you've arrived.'

Kazik was surprised to find two men in their early twenties waiting for him in the hall. He had never met Wacek before, and it was quite obvious that he did not recognise me. Even after I introduced myself he didn't seem to be all that welcoming. But he gave me an important piece of news: 'Your father is running a camp for Polish refugees in Genillet, but he happens to be in Paris today. You can find him in Hôtel des Gobelins, near the Gobelins metro station. You'd better go there straight away,' and he gave me five hundred franks for the fare.

It was only later that I learned that Captain Żupański, the man we'd met the day before in Baden-Baden, had promised to send a car to my uncle. It must have been disappointing to be presented with me instead! Actually, the car never materialised, as three days after our visit at the Żupańskis in Baden-Baden, he and his glamorous wife did a bunk for Canada, so that in fact the good captain hadn't risked anything by signing our passes for Paris; he obviously knew that in a matter of days he would be out of reach of his communist rulers in Warsaw.

We reached Father's hotel at about 9 a.m. 'Mr Likiernik is out,' said the receptionist, 'but Mrs Likiernik is in.' I knew it could not be Mother, whom I had left in Poland, but I was not particularly surprised. After five years of captivity, nature demanded its rights. The Polish widow from the Genillet refugee camp was clearly embarrassed when I introduced myself. 'Your father,' she said, 'had a rendezvous to attend in Café Régence, next to the Comédie Française.'

Once more we had to find our way in a city neither of us knew, but we got there quickly and easily spotted Father in his Polish uniform. The last time I had seen him was in October 1939, at the time of his arrest, when he was fifty-three. Now, at fifty-nine, he looked just the same; perhaps slightly thinner. I, on the other hand, had inevitably changed out of all recognition. I went up to him. He looked at me blankly. '*Dzień dobry*, Good morning,' I said in Polish. Still not a flicker of recognition. Astonished, he looked at me. 'Do I know you?'

'Don't you recognise me?'

Only a minimal negative movement of the head. So I had to introduce myself, as well as Wacek. Father was astounded and delighted at the same time. He had heard that I had survived the war and that I was living in Gdańsk. But postal services were erratic, and it hadn't even occurred to him that I might be seeking him here in Paris.

The man Father was meeting in the café was an employee of the Polish Embassy and they were discussing Father's possible return to Poland. My illegal departure from Poland would not now be the best recommendation . . . Before we left for the camp in Genillet, Father managed to procure documents of former prisoners of war for Wacek and me, as well as the civilian suits and double ration cards to which we were thus entitled.

Paris, and France in general, struck us as a kind of paradise. After the despoiled and ravaged Poland, Warsaw in particular, the amazingly intact city was magnificent and the countryside outstandingly beautiful. Later, in Tours, we felt more at home: the centre of the town had been reduced to rubble by an American carpet-bombing raid. Not a pleasant sight, but so very familiar.

We stayed just a few days in Genillet. One day the village held a great ball. Wacek, popular with the ladies as usual, was the special favourite of our hosts' daughters and I danced the local hairdresser off her feet. We also managed to visit Countess Branicka, the matriarch of the noble Polish family and the grandmother of my friend Ata Branicka-Rybińska. She lived in the magnificent Château de Montrésor, built in the Middle Ages, restored by Count Branicki in 1850 and still owned by the family. I gave her the news of her granddaughter's survival and of the birth of her great-grandson, which she accepted with the indifference of old age.

After this short lull we had to decide on our next move.

Wacek had learned that his father was commanding a Polish Army unit in Jerusalem. In order to join him, Wacek had to get to Italy and enlist in the Second Polish Corps. From there he would have to wangle his way to Palestine. Eventually, he did manage to join his father and was subsequently evacuated with the Polish Army from the Middle East to the UK.

I decided to stay for the time being in Paris and improve my language skills, while reconsidering the problem of returning to

Poland. Wacek and I had to part company. I rented a small room in hotel Gobelins, the site of my first meeting with Father.

My Uncle Kazik and his new wife decided to remain in Paris, but I was not in close contact with them. We did not see eye-to-eye on any subject. Having spent the war years in a prisoner-of-war camp and having lately worked in the Polish Embassy, Kazik was rather out of touch with the reality of life in Poland. It was only later that a brief visit to Warsaw opened his eyes. In the meantime I could not tolerate his views, and his calling the Home Army a fascist movement closed all dialogue between us.

My father's cousin, Antoni Likiernik, the son of Arthur of whom I spoke in the first chapter, commanded a Polish company on guard duty at American army stores. He got me a shirt and a pair of army trousers: I had them altered, and was able to parade in the streets of Paris in the uniform of a Polish second lieutenant. Antoni, though much older than I, became a very good friend. A chemical engineer by profession, he was a successful industrialist before the war. During the years of the German occupation he worked in one of the Home Army underground factories producing explosives, incendiary bottles, etc. In 1946 in Paris, he tried to talk me into writing down my wartime experiences while they were fresh in my mind and, under his influence, I scribbled a few pages during my stay with him, but later my pen gathered dust for many years. He would have been thrilled to hear that I finally followed his advice and had my memoirs published. But he died of a heart attack, aged fifty-eight, at his home in Paris.

At first I was lonely and rather lost on my own in Paris. Then, to improve my French, I enrolled in the *Cours de Civilisation Française* at the Sorbonne, and this was my salvation. At the university I met Jurek, lately of Żolibórz; we became good friends and have remained so to this day. In addition to our common language and culture we shared a passion for oranges and dates, fruit we had not seen through the long years of war. I even sacrificed my ration coupons for tobacco, cheese and meat, in exchange for which the local shopkeeper kept me supplied with the exotic fruit.

One day, entirely by chance, I learned that there were rooms reserved for students at the Cité Universitaire and went there to find out more. I was given an application form, which I then had to hand in, joining a long queue of applicants. I reached the desk of one of the ten girls manning them. The girl looked at me. 'Are you Polish?' she asked, eyeing my uniform. 'My grandfather was Polish too,' she smiled, and put my application form on top of the heap. Within ten days I was assigned a room in the Japanese pavilion, at the time understandably devoid of Japanese. Within days I got to know other students: French, Tunisian and a charming Moroccan Jew. One of my neighbours, a Frenchman from Barcelona, François Gaudillat, undertook the task of teaching me French and helped me in other ways too, but I'll come back to that later.

On my first day in the Cité Universitaire, in April or May 1946, on entering our pavilion I ran into a group of French students discussing something with great passion. It had to be politics – what else could create so much heat? I tried to listen and managed to catch some words, a few bits of sentences. They sounded very strange to me – was it my poor comprehension?: 'Not less than half an hour . . .' 'On rather low heat . . .' 'A twig of rosemary will make all the difference . . .'

I couldn't stand the suspense any longer. 'What are you arguing about?' I asked the boy standing next to me. 'Oh, we can't agree on a weighty matter of cuisine – the best method of preparing rabbit *à la moutarde*, actually.' It was then that the difference between our countries hit me for the first time. It would have been unthinkable to find a group of Polish youths passionately discussing matters pertaining to cuisine. Politics, religion, love, sex, yes, but cooking?

I had known for some time that my friends Roman and Zbyszek had been released from prisoner-of-war camps in Germany and were somewhere in France. Then I heard that Roman returned to Poland, but that Zbyszek remained in Paris. I wrote to Roman asking for Zbyszek's address. Two months later I got his reply. Zbyszek lived in the Cité Universitaire, in the Franco-British pavilion, not a hundred metres away from me!

Delighted, I looked him up straight away and found him equally pleased. Two months ago, he told me, he had overheard a conversation in Polish. He thought he had recognised my voice. But earlier that day he was given a photograph taken a couple of days earlier showing a double of his comrade killed in the Rising. Having known for sure that I survived the war but remained in Poland, he took it for a day of hallucinations and did not bother to check.

We decided to share a room in the Japanese pavilion and stayed together, as good friends, for the next two years. Zbyszek, a poet and a natural born journalist, made his living by writing a satirical column for a Polish newspaper published in Paris. I had no steady work. Earlier on, while it was still possible to send money out of Poland, I had written several pieces, mainly war reminiscences, for a newspaper back home and they were able to forward my fees. I was also engaged in a little trade with Roman. I would send him shoes, sometimes one shoe at a time, to prevent theft. Roman would sell them in Warsaw on the black market and send me the proceeds. Due to a favourable exchange rate I could invest three thousand franks and gain double that amount. My rent being three thousand franks per month, I was able to spend the remainder on food.

In the summer of 1946 far-reaching changes took place in our family life. Father took over the post in the Polish Mission in Baden-Baden vacated by the unexpected departure of Captain Żupański. I spent part of the summer holidays with him, hoping that the magic of the officer's uniform would open some doors for me.

The situation in Poland remained uncertain. By then the communist government, which till now included Mikołajczyk, leader of the Peoples' Party and previously a member of the Polish Government-in-Exile in London, abandoned all pretence of benevolence. Mikołajczyk was ousted by the communists and had to escape once more to the West. The last vestiges of democracy disappeared and the tightening of the screw began in earnest.

Father was still in charge of the Baden-Baden Mission, but its staff was radically changing. The demeanour of the new arrivals from Poland, especially of the officers, was getting increasingly strange. Some communists of Jewish origin could hardly even speak Polish. Others infuriated me by asking stupid questions: had I, for instance, been killing members of the AL during the Rising? Father once dared to point out publicly that democracy could coexist with socialism, as it successfully did in Sweden. Such remarks could only gain him black marks in his dossier.

Other than learning French and doing some horse riding, and in spite of my uniform, I had little to do in Baden-Baden. Many Poles had started affairs with German women, but the war and its memories were too close for me and I wanted no contact with any German, whether in skirts or trousers.

In the beginning of 1947 we were joined by Mother. She arrived with her niece Krysia, a thirteen-year-old orphan. Krysia, whose Jewish parents had been killed in Auschwitz, was saved by a Christian friend of her mother, a Mrs Kozilkiewicz. Leaving Poland had by now become very difficult and people were trying to escape by various clandestine routes. However, Mother managed to get passports for both of them with the help of General Komar, an acquaintance of Father's, and their departure had thus been perfectly legal. The general, a veteran of the International Brigade in the Spanish Civil War, was himself arrested soon after. Our family of three had miraculously survived the war and now we were not only together once more, but had even gained a fourth member.

Of the remaining members of my father's family, his sister, Alina Wojecka, had lost two of her three children. Marie, her only daughter, had disappeared, nobody knew where or how, at the beginning of 1944. Staś, a few years my senior and a medical student at the start of the war, worked as a doctor during the Rising in the makeshift hospital in an Old Town Church. I did not know it at the time, but his hospital was only some three hundred metres from the one where I was a patient. After the hospital was bombed by the Germans, Staś and other survivors were carrying the wounded out of the burning building when the roof fell in, killing them all, staff as well as patients. Only Alina's youngest, Piotr, survived the war. Piotr was some two years older than I. In 1939 he escaped to the east and was taken prisoner by the Russians, interned in the Kozielsk POW camp. In 1940 thousands of inmates of this and other camps were murdered by the NKVD. Miraculously, Piotr happened to be among the four hundred inmates packed in the last train going to the notorious site of the massacre, the Katyń forest, who were, inexplicably, spared. In 1942 he managed to reach the Polish Army reborn in the USSR and fought in the armoured brigade on the Italian front, taking part in the battle of Monte Cassino.

At some stage, having missed a few exams, I left the Sorbonne and found myself once more at a loss. One day my friend François Gaudillat introduced me to his Corsican pal, De La Rocca Serra, a student of the École de Sciences Politiques; in time he would become a Member of the French Parliament in Corsica. It was he who gave me the piece of advice which opened a new chapter in my life. 'You ought to apply to the Sciences Po.,' he said, using the common abbreviation for the famous Parisian college. 'And if you can get the Polish Embassy to certify that you were an officer of the Polish *résistance*, you'll have a good chance of getting in. Who knows? They may even allow you to skip the introductory year.'

This sounded like very good advice. It would give me a definite direction and a starting point for a future career. With the help of my uncle, who at the time was still working for the Polish Embassy, I got the required certificate. An interview with the school's director, Mr Chapsal, was arranged and I became a student of the École de Sciences Politiques.

'It's one thing to be admitted and quite another to graduate,' said my uncle Kazik, sarcastic as usual.

The lectures I attended at the École de Sciences Politiques filled a lot of gaps in my perception of the world and its recent history. During the war I had done my utmost to fight Nazism, but my understanding of all the *isms*, communism, fascism, socialism and the like was, at best, disjointed and hazy; bits of information jumbled in my head like pieces of a jigsaw puzzle. The college offered me an opportunity to fit them all together.

TWENTY-FIVE

Settling In

IT WAS NOT EASY TO FIND ONE'S PLACE in the post-war world, and I was
happy to start the academic year of 1946 as a student of the École de
Sciences Politiques. I was aware that this was a privilege, but
inevitably there were accompanying problems. Most of the students
of my year were French, some five years younger than I. They came
to the École straight from school and had behind them the
introductory year, crowned by the passing of the end-of-year
competitive examination. I had an incomparably greater life
experience but practically no preparation for the kind of study facing
me, added to which was the handicap of having to work in a foreign
language.

With the help of duplicated copies, I followed the lectures
without too much difficulty. Some, like those given by the
celebrated Professor Siegfried on political geography, were
fascinating. But the seminars, in groups of twenty with a lecturer,
were much more difficult: one was expected to speak, to expound
one's views and to present written work. The latter in particular
proved far from easy.

My first essay was on nationalisation and, helped by René
Langlois, one of my new friends in the Japanese pavilion, I put a lot
of effort into it. The finished paper seemed quite good to me.
Reasonably satisfied, I handed it in. On returning it, our seminar
leader roundly berated me, assessing my work as totally worthless.
His attitude gave me a shock and I felt quite resentful. I thought that
the man, who was also the general secretary of the Small Traders
Association, had failed to take into consideration my special status
as a foreigner and an ex-serviceman. He is as small as his traders, I
decided angrily.

In time I came to understand the reason for my failure. The
French school inculcates into its students from their earliest

childhood the notion that all learning must follow a general plan. Coherent structure is all-important in the preparation of a lecture or in any written exercise. In the Sciences Po. *le plan* was a shibboleth, a sacred cow. Without it, no clear expression of thought was deemed possible. A work worth its name had to consist of an introduction, three elegantly interconnected parts and 'a conclusion opening wider perspectives'. The axiom of the French method of teaching was that 'the proof of good understanding of a subject is the ability to present it clearly'. The form is as important as the idea, or so the French think. And this was something I was neither prepared for nor appreciated at the time. The exams at the end of the year were oral and I did reasonably well in them. Now I had to concentrate on improving my written French. The following year became much easier. Our lecturer, Mr Amar, was a highly intelligent man and I found that we were much more on the same wavelength. He even congratulated me on my paper on Political Economy and Economic Policy, an interesting and still highly topical subject, which I wrote this time in accordance with the Sciences Po. rules.

At the time, the financial basis of my existence was precarious, to say the least. My parents, in dire straits themselves, were not able to help. However, I was lucky: the Alumni Association of the Sciences Po. awarded me a loan of 3,000 francs a month, to be repaid after graduation. This covered my rent in the Cité Universitaire. And then my two uncles, Kazik and Antoni, offered to fork out 5,000 francs each a month. I was able to make ends meet.

In the meantime, with Mikołajczyk ousted, the communist takeover was complete and the political situation in Poland changed radically. My father was recalled from Baden-Baden to Berlin and in his absence the Baden-Baden Mission was taken over by a new team sent from Warsaw. I happened to be in Baden-Baden at the time and, anxious about my father being left at the mercy of Soviet authorities in Berlin, I went to see Colonel Poignant, the man in charge at the time of foreign military missions in the French occupation zone in Germany. He received me courteously and was interested to hear about the new staff taking over the Mission. Eventually, after Father returned from Berlin without a job, my parents and Krysia moved to Brussels. Father intended to go into business. He got involved in buying horses for Poland where, in the absence of tractors, the animals were urgently required for work in the fields. However, this didn't work out as expected. He then tried to start an import-export business, but it also failed to get off the ground. There were bills to pay: the rent, Krysia's school fees . . . For a while we even considered returning to Poland, but were dissuaded by Kazik.

Uncle Kazik, still working for the Polish Embassy in Paris, had in the meantime been recalled to Warsaw and went there, in spite of his wife's great misgivings. Unhappy with the new communist reality in Poland, he resurfaced after a while in Paris and told us quite clearly: 'If you go back, Tadeusz will without any doubt be arrested as soon as you cross the border.' He then related what happened on their return journey from Poland. Even though their passports were found to be in perfect order, at the border checkpoint he and his wife were taken off the train and for a considerable length of time were questioned about the activities and whereabouts of my father.

The way back having thus been closed, Father contacted Colonel Poignant, who had by now been appointed director of IRO (International Refugee Organisation) for the French occupation zone in Germany. The colonel found Father a job as IRO director in Haslach, near Offenburg, where he was to take care of the numerous refugees from eastern Europe, people who refused to return to their countries, now under communist rule.

While my parents were still in Brussels I arranged to spend the summer of 1947 with them. This provided me with quite another kind of useful life experience. When I arrived in Brussels our family's total capital stood at fifty US dollars – peanuts, so to speak. Father would go out with only one franc in his pocket, in order to avoid all temptation. As I learned later, suicide was one of the options he seriously considered at the time. Sometimes we would keep our morale up by window shopping and Father would dream aloud: 'That's the motorcycle I shall buy you . . . and this fashionable suit . . . one day, when I will be able to afford it.' At the time Brussels, engorged with money flooding in from the Congo copper mines, suffered no shortages of any kind. Paris, on the other hand, was in economic straits similar to those of Poland, and the consequent austerity was something I was quite used to.

We lived in Brussels in a small flat in Rue Tenbosch. In a neighbouring apartment resided a friendly Polish lady, a survivor of Ravensbrück, one of the most notorious German concentration camps. In spite of her chronic ill health, she worked for a small firm engaged in collecting and sorting waste paper which would subsequently be sold to paper manufacturers. With the good lady's help I joined the enterprise. I had no work permit, but my employer was not averse to exploiting a cheap illegal pair of hands. I joined a team of three men which would bring lorry-loads of bagged waste paper from around the town. The bags varied in weight, but a hundred-kilogram load on one's back was not unusual. My two Flemish companions were used to heavy physical labour, whereas I was new to it. Yet I had to do my share. We had a half-hour lunch break when they would tuck into their thick sandwiches bulging with slices of meat, while I had to make do with dainty canapés, prepared by my mother who had no idea of the demands of back-breaking labour. Having satisfied their first hunger, 'Hey you, student,' one or the other of my two mates would say, 'What are you going to do after university?' This was a question I kept asking myself too and which I was not able to answer. They were full of good advice, mostly pulling my leg in the process.

My work gear consisted of an old American army shirt and trousers and on my head I wore a tatty hairnet to hold my then still abundant thatch. I would get home in the evening tired and filthy. By the time I got rid of the accumulated layers of grime and had eaten my dinner, I was exhausted and fit only for bed.

I was enduring all this in a city whose streets were packed with luxury cars, where shop windows were overflowing with elegant clothes and where the temperature was reaching forty degrees centigrade; the summer of 1947 was the hottest in my experience. I hated Brussels; its riches, its self-important burghers. I was becoming a proletarian and the experience was pushing me inexorably towards the political left, which became my spiritual retreat for the next few years.

Two vignettes are still vivid in my memory. We were collecting bundles of waste paper from the loft of an elegant bourgeois apartment belonging, so I was told, to a renowned surgeon. Among the waste paper I found old, pre-war numbers of the magazine *Art*. I was leafing through one of them and started reading an article on Romanesque architecture. Unexpectedly, the owner appeared next to me. 'Are you interested in art?' he asked, with more than a soupçon of surprise in his voice. Before I had a chance to answer, he added 'That's good,' in a patronising way.

'Yes,' I said. 'I am a student on a temporary job.'

'Where are you studying?'

'At the École de Sciences Politiques, in Paris. Second year.' He could not have been more surprised. At the time, Belgian students used to spend their holidays on much more congenial pursuits.

Another time, on presenting myself for work, our boss told me to stay behind. Once the team had left for their round of Brussels, he turned round to face the basement hall, spread his arms wide and said: 'Isn't it a complete mess?' It was a rhetorical question. He was absolutely right. The hall, actually a big cellar, was chock-a-block with bales of pressed waste paper scattered helter-skelter in a crazy confusion all over the floor and high up against the walls. I had a feeling that the owner had chosen the occasion to give me an opportunity to rest, that he did not expect anything of me. But having been shown the mess I felt suddenly responsible – and while my personal fourth law of thermodynamics was the conservation of energy, i.e. doing as little as one could get away with – there, in that miserable cellar, I didn't spare myself. I worked as never before. Perspiration was running from every pore of my body as if I was in a Turkish bath.

In the evening, when the boss came round, he looked in amazement at the transformation. 'Who has done this?' he asked.

'I did.'

'You? On your own? Impossible!'

It was in this wretched cellar that I learned an important lesson. When given individual responsibility, people work immeasurably better. This lesson stood me in good stead later in life and I applied it over and over again with a great deal of success. I was able to confirm my conclusion when I took on the process of work organisation in the factories of Philips, the electrical equipment firm.

Father, in the meantime, thinking I needed some relaxation, organised horse riding for me in the evenings. One of his friends had a horse he could spare. But though I loved the sport, by the end of the day I was usually so exhausted that I didn't really enjoy it and on some nights couldn't even get round to it.

By the end of August, after six weeks of that grim work, I'd had enough. It was time to move on. By chance I learned that a Belgian aristocrat was organising an international camp for pacifists on his seaside estate. This was bound to be free. I managed to get the details, and was in luck. As a result I spent ten days under canvas on a lovely estate within walking distance of the sea. The camp was truly international and included a great number of Americans, a Texan among them. I had great difficulty in penetrating his drawl, but we more or less managed to understand each other. One day he asked me whether I would like to go to Bruges. 'I have met a girl from there,' he said, 'and I have a standing invitation, but won't be able to go. Would you go in my place?'

Why not? The opportunity was too good to be missed. But when I arrived at the girl's door, I found that she wasn't there. Her parents nevertheless invited me to lunch, after which her father, a late burgomaster of Bruges, took me round that beautiful town whose every stone he knew and loved. I spent a lovely afternoon in Bruges. In the evening I asked my Texan friend how he got to know the family. 'I met the girl on a train, coming here from Brussels,' he said. 'We chatted and she gave me her address. I haven't seen her since.' As the whole journey from Brussels took all of forty-five minutes, theirs was but a brief encounter.

The holidays over, I returned to the Cité Universitaire. We were due for our annual medical examination. I went with René Langlois, my neighbour in the Japanese pavilion. 'I don't like it,' said René. 'Who knows what they might find?'

'Stop playing Cassandra,' I said laughing. 'We are young, we are fit. Nothing to worry about.'

After the examination, the doctor asked me to wait. He wanted a word with me. Suddenly I became anxious. He noticed it and added, 'We have to do further tests. An X-ray, blood tests. You have a patch on the lung just under the right collar bone. Could be tuberculosis.'

It was a bolt from the blue. A chum of René, a second-year medical student, happened to be passing by. I waylaid him: 'Listen, one of my friends was found to have a patch on the lung. Just under the clavicle. What could it be?'

'It might get serious, unless promptly treated.'

In the evening Zbyszek came to my room. He found me lying on top of my bed. I was feeling very low and envisaging the worst. The medical student I had spoken to before managed to ease my way into his hospital for tomography; it was a new radiological technique giving pictures of the chest in successive slices. On the first slice, his professor found an enormous cavity. The next slice showed that the cavity was, in fact, much smaller – it seemed to be rapidly diminishing in size. The last slice showed that actually there was no cavity at all but a fragment of metal, a piece of shrapnel from August 1944. Its shadow was giving the appearance of a cavity. The professor was delighted. Needless to say so was I, as were my friends, no longer at risk due to contact with me. My case was published in a medical journal, under the heading: '*Sur l'écho d'un éclat d'obus simulant une caverne au poumon,*'or 'On the shadow of a grenade fragment masquerading as a pulmonary cavity.'

My encounter with pulmonary tuberculosis, then, had a prompt and happy ending. There was one positive sequel in that I was given a pass to the special canteen for convalescent students. The food there was incomparably better than in Cité Universitaire: large amounts of milk, cheese etc., which in no time restored my equilibrium. Though no longer could I play on the sympathy of my friends as another Pole suffering with tuberculosis, practically another Chopin – too bad that I was musically illiterate but, unlike Chopin, I survived beyond my forty-ninth year.

I did not have all that many friends among the students. A great majority of them were much younger than I, and we had very little in common. Although I was still in uniform, it was unfortunately a Polish one, not the popular American or Canadian, associated in peoples' minds with money, cigarettes and chocolates. Because of this I also missed out on the distinctive Sciences Po. fashion: a black hat and a mandatory tie, both of which were part of the fashionably snobbish way of expressing oneself. This was not the kind of lifestyle likely to appeal to an old campaigner after five years of war. One particular event illustrated the problem rather well. Sciences Po. was organising the first post-war ball. Dinner jacket and black tie were *de rigueur*. I was asked by one of the girls whether I intended to go. 'No,' I answered. 'Naturally, I have a dinner jacket, but in solidarity with those who haven't I decided not to go.'

She didn't understand the irony. She thought it was a great gesture. 'It's really good of you,' she said.

TWENTY–SIX

Annie

A PACKED LECTURE THEATRE WAS THE RULE IN PARIS, but giving up seats to latecomers of the fair sex was not. However, with my Polish upbringing still second nature, I would without a moment's hesitation get up and invite any tardy female to take my seat. This act of old-fashioned chivalry was usually rewarded with a heart-warming smile and that was how, one day, I got to know Lizon Maury, a girl from Auch in Gascony. Lizon was not a beauty, but was a lively and likeable person. We would often leave class together, only to part company soon after – she on her way to a café at Saint-Germain-des-Prês and I up the Sainte-Genevieve hill to Saint Ginette, the students' restaurant, next to the Pantheon. For some reason I assumed that the café she frequented belonged to her family.

After the Brussels holiday, at the start of the new academic year, I ran into Lizon. She greeted me with her usual friendly smile, congratulating me on the good marks in my oral exams. I liked Lizon but had never flirted with her; we usually spoke about the university, gossiped about lectures, lecturers, colleagues.

One November day in 1947, I was crossing the Gay-Lussac street and noticed Lizon crossing the road in the opposite direction, a short distance away from me. But she was not alone. She was in animated conversation with another girl, a very pretty brunette, who immediately caught my eye. I turned round and ran after them, using some lecture notes Lizon had promised me as a pretext.

I was introduced in this way to her friend, Annie Dupouy, and learned that the two girls were sharing a room in the Hôtel de l'Observatoire on the Boulevard Saint-Michel, and that they met every day for lunch in the café next to the Diderot monument. In that instant I resolved to get to know Annie better. My platonic friendship with Lizon would not be an impediment. I learned later that Annie had already heard about me from Lizon, but for some reason had expected me to be much taller than in fact I was. To follow my intention through, I invited both girls to a dance in the Cité Universitaire. Annie and I were both twenty-four years of age, and this was the beginning of a life-long commitment.

I was not able to introduce Annie to my parents who were still in Haslach, in the French zone of occupation in Germany, but Uncle Kazik was to meet my fiancée *in loco parentis*. He also decided to put to the test his conviction that Polish men invariably fell for the wrong French women: vamps and coquettes. He invited us to dinner. Much as it went against my habits, I remained silent and let Annie and Kazik monopolise the conversation between them. It was lively and never flagged, and the word 'vamp' never came up again.

In July 1948 I took Annie to meet my parents for the first time. With Krysia, they lived in a large villa in Haslach. The villa belonged to a German called Armbruster, whose role was now that of handyman and gardener. In his dealings with us he was obsequiously attentive, even servile. He expressed contempt for all the other victorious nations: the French were dirty, the English were hypocrites; but in our presence he would not fault Poles in any way. The temperature of our relations, never warm, dropped to below freezing when one day he proudly showed me a photograph of his late son in an SS uniform. The young man was killed in Russia, but I was not able to commiserate with his father. Armbruster never understood why I had no further appetite for his memorabilia.

My parents took to Annie straight away, and approved of my choice without hesitation; and with good reason. Annie was very attractive and intelligent, but modest with it, as well as which she had a very pleasant manner. We decided to get married in September in Montferran-Savès near Toulouse, where Annie's parents, both of them teachers, lived and worked.

Before the wedding I spent five weeks in a students' camp in England helping with the harvest. I needed to earn some money and wanted to improve my English. In Great Britain of 1948 there were shortages of food and labour was scarce, yet my first application for a place in the camp, sent from France, had been refused and only the second one, sent by Wacek Koc from his Oxford address, was accepted. Consequently, I was the only foreigner in the camp near Droitwich. It certainly was a good way to polish up my English.

In the meantime, Annie went to Montferran-Savès to deal with the preliminaries of our wedding and, no doubt, to gently prepare her parents and generally pave the way for her exotic fiancé.

In August 1948 I went to stay in London with my cousin Danuta, Kazik's daughter, and her brand new husband, Stefan. It was Danuta's and my first meeting since 1939. She and Stefan, with their respective families, had spent the early years of the war in the USSR and had met on leaving that country in 1942. Danuta was at first in Tel-Aviv, where she attended the Polish high school. She then joined the Polish Red Cross in Italy together with her mother. Stefan had fought in the ranks of the Polish Second Corps, part of the British Eighth Army, in Italy. Their deportation, separately, into the depths of the USSR, Stefan's work as a lumberjack in a Siberian forest, and their meeting on the shores of the Caspian Sea is a long and interesting story described by them jointly in Stefan's book *The Ice Road*, published in 1999 (Mainstream Publishing). Taken together, our reminiscences, the story of only one family, illustrate a large part of the wartime history of the Polish people.

The England I visited in 1948 was a country very different from either Poland or France. Our work on bringing in the cereal harvest, on cabbage planting etc, was heavy and tiring but on the whole, I would imagine, much the same as anywhere else. But the food! Oh, the food was something quite indescribable! Porridge and kippers for breakfast – just imagine smoked fish for *petit déjeuner* – lunch consisted of two slices of cotton wool-like bread with a leaf of lettuce, devoid of any dressing, between them. Some other unmentionable mess for dinner. The agony of it!

At the time Great Britain still jealously guarded her insularity and maintained her separateness, and I could not get over the quaint manners of the British. Once, when I expressed my impatience while waiting in a long queue for a railway ticket, I was stared at as if I were an escaped lunatic. Another time, while recalling at the dinner table the discovery of an old castle in the neighbourhood, I pointed out the direction with my finger. It was greeted with general laughter. My pointing finger was apparently shockingly 'continental'; the correct description would have been something like 'to the south-west from here'. Good God, did I have to walk everywhere with a compass in my hand? On top of it, everybody had known about the castle, but nobody volunteered the information. Why? 'You never asked. We couldn't possibly impose . . .'

Towards the end of another day spent on tying sheaves of wheat full of prickly thistles, somebody suggested a walk to a nearby village. A local party? A chance to relax, perhaps to dance! After an hour's march we arrived at a pub. It looked promising. My English friends ordered pints of beer, repeated the order and kept emptying them one by one. Not being partial to beer I didn't order any, and waited for the real entertainment to begin. But nothing happened. That was all – just beer. One hour's walk, five or six kilometres each way, for that. Never again would I be tempted by this treat.

❧

On my way back to France I stopped again in London and visited the British Museum and some London parks. From Paris, I proceeded south to Toulouse and Auch. It was 4 September 1948.

I arrived in Toulouse at 5 a.m. and changed trains for Auch. In the local train, to my great surprise, I was the only man in the car without a shotgun. Was there a peasant uprising? No, it was just the first day of the hunting season. That day, in Gers, hunters must have been thicker on the ground than rabbits. I was impressed with the number of guns; we could have done with them back home, during the Uprising.

I disembarked at a small station some three kilometres from Montferran-Savès. Annie was waiting for me with a bicycle on which to load my suitcase. Her father sent his excuses, but the attractions of the first day of the hunting season proved stronger than his curiosity to meet his future son-in-law.

We had two days to fill before the wedding, and during that time I met most of Annie's extended family. They were all a little apprehensive of this foreigner who spoke French with a peculiar accent, so very unlike the local one. Borrowing my future father-in-law's bicycle was part of my false start. I set out to explore the area, but cycled straight into a field of prickly weeds and managed to puncture both tyres. The episode didn't endear me to Annie's father, a bit of a pedant who took meticulous care of his belongings.

But this was just the beginning.

At last the great day came. My parents had planned to join us, but their application for French visas had been rejected. Consequently we settled for a very modest affair, without even the participation of Annie's numerous aunts and uncles. It was all very simple. The Mayor's offices and the school, where Annie's parents taught and lived, were all in one building, so that the whole celebration took place under the same roof. The Mayor, Mr Maté, had known Annie all her life and would have been expected to speak first. But he didn't, apparently intimidated by the presence of Annie's father, *Monsieur l'Instituteur*, who tended to look down on him.

The formal ceremony ended and we sat down to dinner. We were ten celebrants in all, including Annie's grandmother, Jeanne, a tiny lady dressed all in black. The wedding feast started with *pâté de foie gras*, a delicacy I had never even heard of before. In addition, there was a dish of ordinary *pâté*. I praised the latter in preference to the former, which was by far too delicate for my mid-European taste buds. Obviously an acquired taste, which I had as yet failed to acquire. This was gaffe number one.

During the meal Annie's father produced from his cellar a bottle of old claret, which had been waiting over twenty years for his only daughter's wedding. He carried it in with great ceremony and piously placed it on the sideboard. In an attempt to expiate my first *faux pas*, I blundered into another. Picking up and raising a wineglass to my lips I remarked, 'What an excellent old claret.' Gaffe number two! It was a good table wine, but it wasn't the old claret. Damnation! But how the hell was I supposed to know?

The behaviour of the 'barbarian from the East' got Annie's father visibly worried. *La cuisine* played a very important role in Gascony in general and in the life of the Dupouy family in particular. After the last course – do I dare call it pudding? – which, like the entire meal, was excellent, the time came for the Armagnac. Now Armagnac, the pride of Gascony, is drunk from special balloon glasses, shaped to fit snugly into the palm of the hand. The glass-holding hand is supposed to execute a number of circular movements so as to make the contents of the glass flow round and round and get gently warmed in the process. Only then is one meant to savour its bouquet and relish its taste, in small mouthfuls taken at suitable intervals. But having been already branded a barbarian I had nothing to lose. I decided to shock my audience, and in the Polish vodka-drinking way I emptied my glass in one gulp.

My reputation was thus sealed. No one in Montferran-Savès has since spoken to me about *la cuisine*, spirits, wines or vintages . . . Thank God for that.

I have no doubt that after my performance my father-in-law would have been a much happier man if he could have called the whole ceremony off. But it was too late. Such was the modest beginning of our good life together.

We celebrated our golden wedding in 1998 – in our own way.

Epilogue

AFTER THE WEDDING, having given up the idea of returning to Poland or of emigrating further afield, we decided to make our home in Paris. Life was difficult. We had to pay our way, and also to repay our student loans. The so-called 'thirty years of prosperity' in France were still to come. Annie, a qualified social worker, soon found a suitable job, but I was less successful. In those days, relying on one's wife's earnings was a disgrace. I was unemployed for three months and have never forgotten the shame of it. In Paris at that time any living space, even a room with a leaking roof, cost the earth. Finding accommodation with limited funds was an art. With a long-term United Nations session then taking place in the French capital, even hotels, both expensive and cheap, were full.

Looking for work was a process full of mysteries to me. With no work references, in my naivety I wrote innumerable letters with details of my activity in the Polish Underground, of my officer status and my wartime decorations. I had no idea that information of this kind was of no interest to prospective employers or, in fact, to anybody. These three months were very difficult for me.

One day I happened to pass by Zak's Art Gallery in Place Saint-Germain-de-Prês. In my despair, and on an impulse, I walked in. The gallery was managed by a Mr Reykis, a distant relation of the Zak family which was in turn related to my aunt Alina. I knew the man vaguely and had nothing to lose. And – wonders will never cease – with his help I found work in Arianex, a firm selling office documentation and classification packages, rather sophisticated for the time. I worked there for ten years, nine years too long in my opinion, but there wasn't anything better on offer, though not for the want of trying. During that time my wife gave birth to our daughter, Wanda, in 1953 and son, Jan, in 1957.

As I had left Poland illegally, contact with my friends who had remained there had to be restricted to correspondence. Afraid of arrest on a trumped up charge of espionage or some other anti-state activity, I didn't dare visit Warsaw. Generally speaking I shared my friends' views on the problems of social justice, on the agrarian reform so badly needed in Poland, etc. In time many of them became writers and journalists, and quite a few came to accept the communist regime under which they had to live. I was not persuaded and the events in Hungary and Czechoslovakia brought my misgivings into even sharper focus. On the other hand, though I had chosen to live under the capitalist system, it did not mean that I admired all of it and the lack of social justice continued to bother me greatly.

Suddenly, in 1956, three years after the death of Stalin, the Polish government relaxed its grip on the population of the country and travel became possible again. I obtained a French passport and, in spite of my father's misgivings, Annie and I decided to visit Warsaw. We travelled in our Citroën 2 CV via Vienna and Bratislava.

At the Czech border checkpoint a Slovak official eyed our documents suspiciously, but on searching our belongings he came across a copy of *Le Canard Enchainé*, a French satirical weekly. Its title page was adorned with a big caricature of General de Gaulle, who had just then come to power in France. Since to an East European official a caricature of a ruler was unthinkable in an official publication, he must have taken us for revolutionaries. He winked and let us through.

At the Polish end of the frontier bridge on the River Odra a crowd of about thirty people were waiting to greet us. Almost all my friends from Warsaw were there with their wives. This wonderful welcome struck a cord in my heart.

At about the same time Roman Mularczyk, under his *nom de plume* of Roman Bratny, published a book entitled *Kolumbowie Rocznik 20* (Columbus Vintage 1920), a novel of the Warsaw Rising, whose combined eponymous character was Stanisław Skiernik, based on Columbus and myself. The book describes a number of the actions of the *Kedyw*.

This was the first publication which dared to present the non-communist Underground in Poland as a positive force. It ended the calumny of the 'Dwarfs of Reaction'. The book proved a great success, and sold a million and a half copies in the next few years. On a more personal level, it made me feel a 'somebody' and after ten years of being the greyest of men *on top of the Paris omnibus* it was a good feeling. The combined shock of being the central character in a book and my warm welcome in Poland was, to me, comparable, *mutatis mutandis*, to the effect the election of a Polish Pope had on the Polish people.

In Warsaw I was in for another shock, namely seeing the Old Town rebuilt. On 30 August 1944, I had left what amounted to one enormous heap of rubble. Now, unbelievably, it looked exactly as it did before the war. Even more beautiful. Lovingly rebuilt in every detail on the basis of old drawings and plans, the original colourful paintings reproduced on the walls, and by now even slightly weathered and covered with the patina of several years. Standing in the Old Town Market I was suddenly overcome by a feeling that the War, the Rising, the destruction, had just been one terrible nightmare.

Traditional Polish hospitality, best described by the common saying: '*Gość w dom, bóg w dom*', or 'When a guest enters your home, God comes into your home', contributed to us being fed to excess. Ten visits a day meant ten full meals and, after a while, even the best of Polish cuisine ceased to tickle the palate. But we enjoyed every minute of our stay in Warsaw, the atmosphere, the old friendships renewed, and the holiday passed only too quickly.

On our return to France it was difficult to settle back into our ordinary life in Paris and into the job I hated. I gave myself three months to find something better. 'Either I'll find it,' I told Annie, 'or I shall remain for ever a nobody in my own eyes.' I thus gambled with my self-esteem and, as so far my numerous attempts to get a better job had failed, this was a risky wager.

However, once more the Grace of God was upon me. I placed a three-line advert in *Le Monde*. This elicited only a single answer, but it was sufficient, as after several interviews I landed the job of deputy director (in charge of organisation and supplies) of a Philips factory. This gave me a great boost and I worked in various departments of the renowned international conglomerate for twenty-five years, until my retirement in 1985.

In time Annie also changed direction. After twenty years as a social worker, she graduated in History of Art from École de Louvre, and for the next seven years worked as guide and lecturer in the Museum of Archaeology in St Germain-en-Laye, close to our new home in Marly-le-Roi in the Versaille area.

So, eventually, we managed to rise in the world and were also able to help support my parents, who in turn looked after our children while we were at work. However, having achieved a reasonable standard of living and the kind of success to which most people aspire, I had to face further problems. After the years of war and occupation, of the constant tension of underground operations with their accompanying risks and dangers, after the challenges of the post-war years and the fight for survival in a foreign country, I found the settled, tranquil life incredibly flat and boring. My French friends could not understand my discontent, my longing for *je ne sais quoi* nor my heartache. But how can a placid horse yoked to his daily work understand one who has spent a large part of his life jumping the highest fences.

However, in time I adjusted to my daily life. Between us, Annie and I brought up our two children, and in time helped to raise our three grandchildren, Wanda's two girls, Carla and Diana, and Jan's boy Anton, the only scion of the Likiernik family. I am still trying to pass on to them some of the lessons I learned during the Second World War: the importance of team work, of the 'one-for-all, all-for-one' variety; not to do to others what you don't want done to yourself; never be afraid; fear is a bad counsel. And my final and most important lesson: liberty is to be valued over anything else, life without freedom is intolerable. This became clear to me in the years of German occupation. Nothing shall erase from my memory the exhilaration of resistance with weapons in one's hands, of bringing the fight to the enemy. Those precious hours or minutes when FREEDOM WAS ALL had been dearer to me than life itself.

Postscript

WACEK KOC did not take part in the Warsaw Rising as he had been assigned to work in the Home Army's Intelligence network in Lwów, as described in previous chapters. Arrested in May 1943, he spent three months in a Lwów prison in terrible conditions. The only times he left the cell was when taken for interrogation. Then, hardly able to walk, he was transferred to the Buchenwald concentration camp. The camp was run with a considerable degree of autonomy by communists, its inmates since the '30s, supervised by the SS. The new arrivals' chances of survival depended on their work assignment. Labour in the quarries or tunnelling the mountains for armament factories meant early death. Chances of survival were better on other placements.

Wacek, exhausted by the conditions in the Lwów prison, was near the end of his tether. He learned only later that he had contracted pulmonary tuberculosis. But luck played a part once more. On his arrival in the camp he came across an old school friend, a member of the communist underground in Warsaw, and thus not without influence in the Buchenwald communist administration. The man, having warned Wacek to keep quiet about his Home Army membership, which his communist friends considered a fascist organisation, secured for him a reasonable work assignment, with a good chance of survival.

However, the last few weeks before the liberation of Buchenwald were very difficult. Most camp inmates had died of starvation and disease. Wacek survived only because of the persistency of German bureaucracy. The authorities insisted that he testify in the case of a Lwów Ukrainian prison guard accused of theft mentioned earlier. Consequently, in the spring of 1945, when the Red Army was already approaching Kraków, Wacek was escorted to Breslau (Wrocław) for the trial.

When the front was approaching Breslau, the prisoners were separated into 'politicals' and 'criminals'. Wacek opted for the latter and survived. The 'politicals' were shot. The 'criminals' were escorted through the town, destination unknown. The man marching next to Wacek suggested running for it. He added, 'I am from around here. I know where to hide.' They found shelter in a thieves' haunt. After two days Wacek started on his way east. He eventually reached Poland and got the job in Sopot. Soon after Wacek and I left Poland, he made his way to the Middle East and was eventually evacuated to the UK with the rest of the Polish Army. He got a degree in history from Oxford, started his own building business and was eventually appointed professor at Lancaster University. Once Poland had shed its communist regime, he returned to Poland. He was about to give a talk on foreign policy to the assembly of the Senate in Warsaw when he collapsed and died of a heart attack.

STASINEK SOSABOWSKI remained in Warsaw's city centre until the day of surrender, 2 October 1945. Because of his serious wounds he was spared imprisonment in a prisoner-of-war camp and soon after the end of the war with the help of his father, General Sosabowski, CO of the Polish Parachute Brigade in the UK, he made his way to England accompanied by his wife and two young sons. Ophthalmic surgery did not succeed in restoring his sight and he trained as a physiotherapist; he worked in one of the London hospitals and in private practice. Eventually the Sosabowski family became British subjects. His children and grandchildren all settled in England and gained university degrees. Stasinek died in November 2000 and I was the only representative of *Kedyw* at his funeral in London.

KRZYSZTOF SOBIESZCZAŃSKI, COLUMBUS also stayed in the city centre until the surrender and was then deported to a prisoner-of-war camp. Released, he stayed in the British zone and, a man of great imagination, he created a fictitious bureau for the recovery of Polish merchant ships stolen by the Germans. Using letter headings of the non-existent office, he smuggled motor cars, in their dozens, to Belgium. In this way he made a fortune, but traced by British police he had to run, lost his fortune and eventually settled in New Zealand. I met him in 1950 in Cannes, in the south of France. He kept spinning grandiose schemes to make another fortune, meeting with varying degrees of success. Experienced sailor though he was, he was caught in a storm sailing in the Mediterranean and drowned.

He left two children in Poland and two in France. One of his sons is a captain in the Polish Navy.

IRKA MINKIEWICZ When I was evacuated from Czerniaków, we lost contact. She thought me dead and didn't learn about my survival until after the war. Released from a prisoner-of-war camp, she trained as a doctor and worked in Poland until 1956 when she emigrated to Australia. She continued her medical career but did not quite settle in her adopted country and kept returning to Europe every few years. She died several years ago.

Of my unit of *Kedyw*, the remaining ten or twelve members continued to fight the Germans for the final three or four days of the Rising, together with the survivors of General Berling's unit (Polish Kościuszko Division under Soviet command) which then, far too late, managed to get across the Vistula. Eventually, the rest of the group, including **JANEK BAGIŃSKI** and **KRYST (CZESLAW KRAŚNIEWSKI)**, both wounded, managed to get across the river under heavy German fire. Of our two nurses, **ZOSIA CZECHOWSKA** and **DANKA MANCEWICZ**, Danka reached the eastern bank but was then wounded. Zosia, the only one who had remained unscathed, helped the wounded onto the Vistula embankment. As always brave and energetic, she managed to get them all to hospital. On their recovery, Janek and Kryst were drafted into the Kościuszko Division and fought under Soviet Command for seven months. On reaching Berlin they had the great satisfaction of seeing the capital of the Reich reduced to ruins.

As the result of the German occupation, of the Warsaw Rising and of the long years of communism, Poland has lost the flower of its population. The Rising alone cost my country some 200,000 lives. Those of Jewish extraction, originally about ten per cent of the population, were mostly killed by the Germans. Further hundreds of thousands failed to return from the concentration camps and prisoner-of-war camps in Germany and similar numbers from the prisons, labour camps and exile in the USSR. Among those who did return from exile in Siberia was my cousin Danuta Szczerba-Likiernik and her husband Stefan Waydenfeld, the joint translators of my memoir into English. Stefan's memoir *The Ice Road* could easily claim the title of my book, as both of us had survived either by the luck of the Devil or by the grace of God, but I claim to have thought of it first.

Translators' Note

The title of this book is not the literal translation of the original Polish title of Stanisław Likiernik's memoir, which would read *By Devil's Luck or By the Grace of God*. In addition to the author's childhood it describes, in the main, events taking place in Warsaw during the German occupation, the people involved, their actions in the Underground army and in the Warsaw Rising. This involves the use of many Polish names, be they streets of the city or the first names, surnames and wartime pseudonyms of the participants. All of those may be difficult and often unpronounceable for the English reader. Some compromise was therefore necessary. We decided to leave the names of streets, towns, city quarters and other geographical names in their original Polish spelling, but either to translate or otherwise explain the names of organisations, institutions, enterprises, etc. As to people, particularly those members of the Underground who are described under both their proper names and pseudonyms, we have endeavoured to specify the surname only occasionally and preferably use either the Christian name or the pseudonym, the latter anglicised where appropriate: e.g. Kolumb is rendered as Columbus, while first names such as Jan, Ryszard etc. are left in their Polish form, rather than artificially translated into English as John or Richard.

As the characters described in this book are real people, and some of them are still alive, we decided to include a brief index listing their real names along with their wartime ones.

Index of Pseudonyms and Names

Andrzej	Andrzej Koc
Antek	Antek Wojciechowski
Antoni	Antoni Tuleja
Ata	Ata Branicka-Rybińska
Bogdan	Bogdan Czapliński
Bor	Zygmunt Siennicki
Budrys	Stanisław Budkiewicz
Columbus	Krzysztof Sobieszczański
Danka	Danuta Babińska
Danusia or Danka	Danuta Mancewicz
Dobrosław	Jan Więckowski
Edmund	Edmund Janiec
Fogel	Maciej Ptaszycki
Halinka	Halina Paschalska
Honorata	Wanda Zalutyńska
Irka	Irena Minkiewicz
Irys	Irena Wnuk
Jaga	Jaga Koc
Jan	Major Andrzejewski
Janek	Jan Barszczewski
Janusz	Janusz Płachtowski
Jerzy	Dr Jerzy Kaczyński
Jodła	Jerzy Krzymowski
Jurek	Jerzy Szwerdykowicz-Kowalewski
Kazik (author's uncle)	Kazimierz Szczerba-Likiernik
Kazik	Kazimierz Jakubowski
Kryst	Czesław Kraśniewski
Morro	Andrzej Romocki
Mundek	Edmund Gurda
Olek	Olek Tyrawski

Olszyna	Wiwatowski
Radosław	Colonel Mazurkiewicz
Remec	Olgierd Cymerski
Renia	Wiączek, wife of Olek Tyrawski
Roman Bratny	Roman Mularczyk
Rysiek	Stanisław Aronsohn
Ryszard	not given
Snica	Bolesław Górecki
Sońka	Włodzimierz Cegłowski
Socha	Jan Bagiński
Stach	Stanisław Czechowski
Staś aka Stach	StaniSław Likiernik, the author
Stasinek	Dr Stanisław Sosabowski
Stefan	Stefan Graf
Trzaska (major)	Major Konopacki
Wacek	Wacek Koc
Zbylut	Witold Piekarski
Zbyszek	Zbigniew Stolarek
Zofia	Zofia Babińska
Zosia C.	Zofia Czechowska
Zosia L.	Zofia Laskowska
Zygmunt	Zygmunt Brzosko